THE SPIRIT OF CHRISTMAS
COOKBOOK
Volume 2

Christmas has its own unique sights, smells, textures, and tastes — and this book is overflowing with everything you need to fill your house with tantalizing aromas, succulent flavors, and elegant-looking foods. Make your selections from exceptional choices like stunning Cranberry Cake decorated with basket weave icing, spicy Gingerbread House Cookies, Hot Buttered Rum Cordial, savory Ginger-Glazed Turkey, or mouth-watering Caramel-Chocolate Layered Fudge — an excellent gift idea. All these delectable dishes and more are included in this second collection of our favorite holiday recipes. This cornucopia of more than 230 kitchen-tested recipes lets you create dishes reminiscent of Grandma's, combine traditional flavors in unconventional ways, or spice up Christmasy fare with tastes from other shores. From parties to presents, from soups to suppers, The Spirit of Christmas Cookbook — Volume 2 *is your source for festive culinary inspiration!*

LEISURE ARTS, INC.
Little Rock, Arkansas

THE SPIRIT OF CHRISTMAS

COOKBOOK

Volume 2

EDITORIAL STAFF

Vice President and Editor-in-Chief: Anne Van Wagner Childs
Executive Director: Sandra Graham Case
Editorial Director: Susan Frantz Wiles
Creative Art Director: Gloria Bearden
Senior Graphics Art Director: Melinda Stout

FOODS
Foods Editor: Celia Fahr Harkey, R.D.
Assistant Foods Editor: Jane Kenner Prather
Test Kitchen Home Economist: Rose Glass Klein
Test Kitchen Coordinator: Nora Faye Taylor
Test Kitchen Assistant: Tanya Harris

EDITORIAL
Managing Editor: Linda L. Trimble
Associate Editors: Robyn Sheffield-Edwards and
 Janice Teipen Wojcik
Editorial Associates: Tammi Williamson Bradley and
 Terri Leming Davidson
Copy Editor: Laura Lee Weland

ART
Book/Magazine Graphics Art Director: Diane M. Hugo
Senior Production Graphics Artist: M. Katherine Yancey
Production Artists: Michael A. Spigner and Guniz Jernigan
Photography Stylists: Karen Smart Hall, Sondra Daniel,
 Christina Tiano Myers, and Charlisa Erwin Parker

PROMOTIONS
Managing Editors: Tena Kelley Vaughn and
 Marjorie Ann Lacy
Associate Editors: Steven M. Cooper, Dixie L. Morris, and
 Jennifer Leigh Ertl
Designer: Dale Rowett
Art Director: Linda Lovette Smart
Production Artist: Leslie Loring Krebs
Publishing Systems Administrator: Cindy Lumpkin
Publishing Systems Assistant: Susan Mary Gray

BUSINESS STAFF

Publisher: Bruce Akin
Vice President, Marketing: Guy A. Crossley
Marketing Manager: Byron L. Taylor
Print Production Manager: Laura Lockhart
Vice President and General Manager: Thomas L. Carlisle
Retail Sales Director: Richard Tignor

Vice President, Retail Marketing: Pam Stebbins
Retail Customer Services Director: Margaret Sweetin
Retail Customer Services Manager: Carolyn Pruss
General Merchandise Manager: Russ Barnett
Vice President, Finance: Tom Siebenmorgen
Distribution Director: Ed M. Strackbein

We would like to extend our thanks to Christy Kalder, Micah McConnell, Susan Warren Reeves, R.D., and Kay Wright for their contributions as former foods editors and consultants for *The Spirit of Christmas* and *Memories in the Making* volumes from which we chose our recipes.

Library of Congress Catalog Card Number 97-73650
International Standard Book Number 0-8487-4160-9

TABLE OF CONTENTS

TABLE OF CONTENTS
(Continued)

TABLE OF CONTENTS
(Continued)

MERRY BRUNCH

*O*ur mid-morning festival of foods will get Christmas Day — or any day during the holidays — off to a very merry start! Whether you serve a hearty breakfast or a light brunch, these delicious dishes are sure to please. You'll discover satisfying foods the whole family will enjoy, from homestyle favorites such as French toast and waffles to more exotic cuisine, including a cheesy strata and seasoned rice pilaf.

Baked with a swirl of nutty cinnamon filling, Walnut Coffee Cake (recipe on page 8) is generously topped with nuts and a sweet glaze.

WALNUT COFFEE CAKE

(Shown on pages 6 and 7)

FILLING

- 1 cup chopped walnuts
- 2 tablespoons sugar
- 1/2 teaspoon ground cinnamon

CAKE

- 1 cup butter or margarine, softened
- 2 cups sugar
- 2 eggs
- 1/2 cup milk
- 1 1/2 cups all-purpose flour
- 1 1/2 teaspoons baking powder
- 1/2 teaspoon salt
- 1 cup sour cream
- 1/2 teaspoon vanilla extract

GLAZE

- 3/4 cup sifted confectioners sugar
- 1 tablespoon butter or margarine, melted
- 1 tablespoon milk
- 1 teaspoon vanilla extract
- 1/2 cup chopped walnuts

Preheat oven to 350 degrees. For filling, combine walnuts, sugar, and cinnamon in a small bowl.

For cake, cream butter and sugar in a large bowl until fluffy. Add eggs and milk; beat until smooth. Sift flour, baking powder, and salt into a medium bowl. Gradually add dry ingredients to creamed mixture, beating until well blended. Beat in sour cream and vanilla. Spoon half of batter into a greased and floured 10-inch tube pan. Spoon filling evenly over batter in pan. Spoon remaining batter over filling; swirl with a knife. Bake 1 hour to 1 hour 15 minutes, testing for doneness with a toothpick. Cool 10 minutes in pan. Remove from pan and cool completely on a wire rack.

For glaze, combine confectioners sugar and butter in a small bowl. Add milk and vanilla; stir until smooth. Drizzle glaze over cake. Sprinkle walnuts over glaze.
Yield: about 16 servings

BACON-WALNUT BISCUITS

- 14 slices bacon, cooked
- 2 cups all-purpose flour
- 2 teaspoons baking powder
- 1/2 teaspoon baking soda
- 1/2 teaspoon salt
- 1/4 cup butter or margarine, cut into pieces
- 3/4 cup finely ground walnuts
- 1 cup whipping cream

Preheat oven to 450 degrees. Process bacon in a food processor until finely chopped. In a large bowl, combine flour, baking powder, baking soda, and salt. Using a pastry blender or 2 knives, cut butter into dry ingredients until mixture resembles coarse meal. Stir in walnuts and bacon. Add whipping cream; stir until a soft dough forms. Turn dough onto a lightly floured surface and knead 1 to 2 minutes or until smooth. Using a lightly floured rolling pin, roll out dough to 1/2-inch thickness. Use desired cookie cutters to cut out biscuits. Transfer to a greased baking sheet. Bake 8 to 10 minutes or until light brown. Serve warm.
Yield: about 2 1/2 dozen 3-inch biscuits

SPICY TOMATO PUNCH

Spicy Tomato Punch may be made one day in advance.

- 4 cups tomato juice
- 1 cup pineapple juice
- 1 cup orange juice
- 2 tablespoons prepared horseradish
- 1 teaspoon ground black pepper
- 1 teaspoon Worcestershire sauce
- 1 teaspoon hot pepper sauce
  Celery stalks to garnish

In a 2-quart container, combine tomato juice, pineapple juice, orange juice, horseradish, black pepper, Worcestershire sauce, and pepper sauce; stir until well blended. Cover and refrigerate 8 hours or overnight to allow flavors to blend. Serve chilled with celery stalks.
Yield: about 6 cups punch

CREAM CHEESE OMELET

- 6 eggs
- 4 ounces cream cheese, softened
- 1 teaspoon salt
- 1/2 teaspoon ground black pepper
- 1 1/2 tablespoons butter or margarine
- 6 green onions, finely chopped

In a large bowl, beat eggs, cream cheese, salt, and pepper using an electric mixer. In a large skillet, melt butter over medium heat. Add green onions; sauté until tender. Pour egg mixture into skillet; stir once to mix egg mixture with onions. Cook 3 to 5 minutes or until top is bubbly and edges begin to brown. Using a knife, lift edges of omelet up and tilt skillet to allow egg mixture in center of omelet to run under omelet. Cook 1 minute longer. Use a spatula to fold omelet in half. Reduce heat to low and cook 3 to 5 minutes longer or until omelet is set in center. Transfer to a warm plate, cover, and place in a 200-degree oven until ready to serve. Serve warm.
Yield: about 3 servings

Omelet lovers will ooh and aah over this light, fluffy Cream Cheese Omelet. Bacon-Walnut Biscuits are great for munching alone or as a breakfast accompaniment, and Spicy Tomato Punch is a break from the usual breakfast drink.

CRANBERRY-BLUE CHEESE SALAD

2 cans (8 ounces each) pineapple tidbits, undrained
1 can (16 ounces) whole berry cranberry sauce
1 package (6 ounces) raspberry gelatin
1/3 cup plus 2 tablespoons cream sherry, divided
3 ounces blue cheese, crumbled and divided
1/2 very ripe banana, mashed
1 teaspoon freshly squeezed lemon juice
1/2 cup whipping cream
2 ounces cream cheese, softened
Orange peel to garnish

Place a small bowl and beaters from an electric mixer in freezer until well chilled. Place pineapple and cranberry sauce in a medium saucepan; bring to a boil. Remove from heat; add gelatin and stir until gelatin dissolves. Cool 5 minutes. Stir in 1/3 cup sherry and 2 ounces blue cheese. Pour into an oiled 6-cup mold, cover, and refrigerate until firm.

In a small bowl, combine banana and lemon juice. In chilled bowl, beat whipping cream and cream cheese until stiff peaks form. Beat in remaining 2 tablespoons sherry and 1 ounce blue cheese. Beat in banana mixture. Cover and refrigerate until ready to serve.

To serve, dip bottom of mold into hot water; invert onto a serving plate. Spoon banana mixture over gelatin. Garnish with orange peel.
Yield: about 12 servings

Chock-full of pineapple tidbits, Cranberry-Blue Cheese Salad features an unusual blend of flavors. Crunchy granola, mellow fruit, and a mixture of cream cheese and yogurt are layered to create these wonderful low-fat Granola-Fruit Parfaits.

GRANOLA-FRUIT PARFAITS

2 cups low-fat granola cereal
4 kiwi fruit, peeled and cut into pieces
1 can (20 ounces) pineapple chunks, well drained
1 package (8 ounces) fat-free cream cheese, softened
1 cup fat-free vanilla yogurt

Spoon half of granola into 6 parfait glasses. Arrange half of kiwi fruit and pineapple over granola. Repeat layers with remaining granola and fruit.

In a small bowl, beat cream cheese and yogurt until smooth. Cover cream cheese mixture and parfaits and refrigerate until ready to serve.

To serve, spoon cream cheese mixture over parfaits.
Yield: 6 servings

A confetti of color, Rice and Barley Pilaf is flavored with bacon and chicken broth. Tender, juicy Peppered Ham is coated with coarse ground pepper and a tangy honey-mustard sauce.

PEPPERED HAM

    4 pound fully cooked boneless
       ham
 1/4 cup honey
    2 tablespoons prepared mustard
    1 clove garlic, minced
    3 tablespoons coarse ground
       black pepper
 1/8 teaspoon ground cloves

Preheat oven to 325 degrees. Place ham on a rack in a shallow roasting pan. In a small bowl, combine honey, mustard, garlic, pepper, and cloves. Brush honey mixture over ham. Loosely cover ham with aluminum foil. Bake 13/4 to 21/4 hours or until heated through. Serve warm.
Yield: about 14 servings

RICE AND BARLEY PILAF

    6 slices bacon
    1 medium onion, chopped
 1/2 cup chopped celery
    2 cans (16 ounces each) chicken
       broth
    1 cup uncooked brown rice
    1 cup uncooked barley
    1 package (10 ounces) frozen
       green peas
    2 medium carrots, shredded
 1/4 cup cooking sherry
 3/4 teaspoon ground turmeric
 1/2 teaspoon ground black pepper
    1 bay leaf

In a large skillet over medium-high heat, cook bacon until crisp. Reserving drippings, remove bacon from pan; set bacon aside. Add onion and celery to bacon drippings; cook until barely tender, stirring frequently. Remove onion mixture from pan and set aside. In same skillet, combine chicken broth, rice, and barley. Cover and cook over medium-low heat 45 minutes or until most of liquid is absorbed. Stir in onion mixture, peas, carrots, sherry, turmeric, pepper, and bay leaf. Reduce heat to low; simmer 10 minutes or until peas are crisp-tender. Remove bay leaf. Crumble bacon on top of pilaf; serve warm.
Yield: 15 to 18 servings

12

FETA CHEESECAKE

CRUST
- 3/4 cup plain bread crumbs
- 3/4 cup finely ground walnuts
- 1 teaspoon dried oregano leaves
- 5 tablespoons butter or margarine, melted

FILLING
- 2 packages (8 ounces each) cream cheese, softened
- 3/4 cup sour cream
- 2 tablespoons all-purpose flour
- 1/2 teaspoon garlic powder
- 1/4 teaspoon hot pepper sauce
- 4 eggs
- 14 ounces feta cheese, crumbled
  Chopped tomato and walnuts to garnish

Preheat oven to 375 degrees. For crust, combine bread crumbs, walnuts, and oregano in a medium bowl. Stir in melted butter; mix until crumbly. Press mixture into bottom of a greased 9-inch springform pan; set aside.

For filling, beat cream cheese, sour cream, flour, garlic powder, and pepper sauce in a large bowl. Add eggs, 1 at a time, beating well after each addition. Stir in feta cheese. Pour into crust. Bake 35 to 40 minutes or until set in center. Cool in pan 10 minutes; remove sides of pan. Garnish with tomato and walnuts. Serve warm.

Yield: 10 to 12 servings

Zesty Feta Cheesecake proves that cheesecake isn't just for dessert anymore! Hearty Cheese Grits Casserole will win new fans for a Southern staple. Chicken Salad in Pastry features a creamy filling and Cheddar-flavored pastry shells.

CHICKEN SALAD IN PASTRY

PASTRY
- 1 cup (4 ounces) shredded sharp Cheddar cheese
- 1/2 cup butter or margarine, softened
- 1 1/4 cups all-purpose flour
- 1/2 teaspoon salt
- 1/4 teaspoon ground black pepper
- 1/4 teaspoon hot pepper sauce

CHICKEN SALAD
- 2 cans (5 ounces each) chicken, drained
- 1 package (3 ounces) cream cheese, softened
- 1/3 cup sour cream
- 1/4 cup finely chopped celery
- 1 hard-cooked egg, finely chopped
- 1/4 teaspoon salt
- 1/4 teaspoon ground black pepper
  Chopped chives to garnish

Preheat oven to 350 degrees. For pastry, combine cheese and butter in a medium bowl. Add flour, salt, black pepper, and pepper sauce; mix until well blended and crumbly. Knead in bowl until a soft dough forms. Using 1 tablespoon of dough for each ball, shape dough into 18 balls. Press balls of dough into bottoms and up sides of 18 well-greased 2 1/2-inch tart pans. Prick sides and bottoms with a fork. Bake 20 to 25 minutes or until lightly browned. Cool in pans 10 minutes. Carefully remove pastries from pans and cool completely on a wire rack.

For chicken salad, combine chicken, cream cheese, sour cream, celery, egg, salt, and pepper in a medium bowl. Cover and refrigerate until ready to serve.

To serve, spoon about 1 tablespoon chicken salad into each pastry. Garnish with chives.

Yield: 1 1/2 dozen pastries

CHEESE GRITS CASSEROLE

- 2 cups milk
- 1 cup water
- 3/4 cup quick-cooking grits
- 3 eggs, beaten
- 1/2 cup (2 ounces) shredded sharp Cheddar cheese
- 3 tablespoons butter or margarine
- 1/4 teaspoon salt
- 1/4 teaspoon ground red pepper
- 4 ounces cooked ham, finely diced
  Sweet red pepper and fresh parsley to garnish

Preheat oven to 350 degrees. In a medium saucepan, bring milk and water to a boil over medium heat. Stir in grits. Bring to a boil again and reduce heat to medium-low. Cook, stirring occasionally, 5 to 7 minutes or until thick. Remove from heat and add eggs, cheese, butter, salt, and red pepper; stir until well blended. Stir in ham. Pour into a greased 1 1/2-quart baking dish. Bake 30 to 40 minutes or until top is set and lightly puffed. (We baked our casserole in a tree-shaped ceramic baking dish 50 to 55 minutes or until edges were lightly browned. It was cooled in dish 10 minutes and inverted onto a serving plate. We used a star-shaped aspic cutter to cut stars from sweet red pepper.) Garnish with red pepper and parsley. Serve warm.

Yield: about 8 servings

STRAWBERRY-FILLED FRENCH TOAST

FILLING

2 packages (8 ounces each)
  cream cheese, softened
½ cup sugar
1 package (16 ounces) frozen
  unsweetened strawberries,
  thawed and drained
1 tablespoon vanilla extract
½ teaspoon ground cinnamon

FRENCH TOAST

11 eggs
½ cup milk
½ teaspoon salt
  Butter or margarine
24 slices white bread
  Confectioners sugar

For filling, beat cream cheese and sugar until fluffy. Add strawberries, vanilla, and cinnamon; stir until well blended.

For French toast, whisk eggs, milk, and salt together until foamy. Melt 1 tablespoon butter in a large skillet over medium heat. For each serving, dip 1 slice bread in egg mixture, turn once to coat, and place in skillet. Spoon about ¼ cup filling in center of bread. Dip another slice of bread in egg mixture, turn once to coat, and place over filling. Cook 3 to 4 minutes or until underside is lightly browned. Turn and cook 3 to 4 minutes longer or until other side is lightly browned. Transfer to a warm plate, cover with aluminum foil, and place in a 200-degree oven until ready to serve. Add butter to skillet as necessary between batches. To serve, dust each piece of French toast with confectioners sugar.
Yield: 12 servings

Strawberry-Filled French Toast is a double-delicious treat with a creamy filling. Frozen Pineapple Salad blends ice cream and sour cream with pineapple and walnuts for a yummy dish.

14

Created with fresh vegetables, spicy Italian sausage, and eggs, Italian Sausage Frittata is a filling breakfast casserole.

FROZEN PINEAPPLE SALAD

  1 can (20 ounces) crushed
      pineapple, drained
1 1/2 cups softened vanilla ice cream
1 1/2 cups sugar
  1 cup sour cream
  1 cup chopped walnuts
  2 tablespoons freshly squeezed
      lemon juice
  1 can (8 ounces) pineapple
      chunks, drained to garnish

In a large bowl, combine
pineapple, ice cream, sugar, sour
cream, walnuts, and lemon juice.
Spoon salad evenly into 8 custard
cups, cover, and freeze 8 hours or
until firm. Before serving, place in
refrigerator 1 hour. Garnish with
pineapple chunks. Serve chilled.
Yield: 8 servings

ITALIAN SAUSAGE FRITTATA

  1 small onion, thinly sliced
  1 medium potato, peeled and
      thinly sliced
  1 pound Italian sausage, cooked
      and crumbled
  3 ounces fresh mushrooms, sliced
  1 small zucchini, thinly sliced
  1 small sweet red pepper, sliced
      into rings
12 eggs, beaten
1/3 cup freshly shredded Parmesan
      cheese

Preheat oven to 350 degrees. In a
greased 12-inch ovenproof skillet,
layer onion, potato, crumbled sausage,
mushrooms, zucchini, and red

pepper. Pour eggs over vegetables;
sprinkle cheese over eggs. Bake
40 to 45 minutes or until eggs are
almost set. Place skillet under broiler;
broil about 3 minutes or until edges
are lightly browned. Cut into wedges
and serve immediately.
Yield: 8 to 10 servings

APPLE-PEAR SKILLET CAKE

    1 cup firmly packed brown sugar
    6 tablespoons butter or margarine,
        cut into pieces
    1 medium unpeeled baking apple,
        cored and sliced
    1 medium unpeeled pear, cored
        and sliced
1 1/3 cups all-purpose flour
    1 cup granulated sugar
    2 teaspoons ground cinnamon
1 1/4 teaspoons baking soda
  1/2 teaspoon salt
    2 eggs
  1/2 cup sour cream
    2 tablespoons vegetable oil
    1 teaspoon vanilla extract

Preheat oven to 350 degrees.
Place brown sugar and butter in a
10 1/2-inch cast-iron or ovenproof
skillet. Place skillet in oven about
5 minutes or until butter melts.
Remove skillet from oven and whisk
brown sugar mixture until well
blended. Arrange fruit slices over
brown sugar mixture. In a medium
bowl, combine flour, granulated
sugar, cinnamon, baking soda, and
salt. In a small bowl, whisk eggs,
sour cream, oil, and vanilla; beat into
flour mixture. Pour batter over fruit;
bake 30 to 35 minutes or until a
toothpick inserted in center of cake
comes out clean. Remove from oven
and place on a wire rack to cool
10 minutes. Run knife around edge of
cake; invert onto a serving plate.
Serve warm.
Yield: about 12 servings

MINTY FRUIT SALAD

    1 jar (10 ounces) whole
        maraschino cherries
    6 oranges, peeled and chopped
    3 bananas, peeled and sliced
  1/2 cup pomegranate seeds
  1/4 cup chopped fresh mint leaves
    2 tablespoons honey
        Fresh mint leaves to garnish

Fresh fruit and a buttery brown sugar topping make Apple-Pear Skillet Cake a sumptuous upside-down treat. It's best when prepared in a cast-iron skillet.

16

Drain cherries, reserving juice. In a large bowl, combine cherries, oranges, bananas, pomegranate seeds, and chopped mint. In a small bowl, combine reserved cherry juice and honey. Pour honey mixture over fruit; stir until well coated. Garnish with mint leaves. Serve chilled.

Yield: about six 1-cup servings

MUSHROOM PIE

CRUST

1½ cups all-purpose flour
½ teaspoon salt
½ cup vegetable shortening
¼ cup cold water

FILLING

½ cup butter or margarine
½ cup chopped green onions
3 cloves garlic, minced
10 ounces fresh mushrooms, sliced
2 cups shredded Swiss cheese
3 eggs
1⅓ cups whipping cream
1 teaspoon dried basil leaves, crushed
1 teaspoon dried thyme leaves, crushed
1 teaspoon salt
½ teaspoon ground black pepper

Preheat oven to 450 degrees. For crust, combine flour and salt in a medium bowl. Using a pastry blender or 2 knives, cut shortening into dry ingredients until mixture resembles coarse meal. Sprinkle with water; mix until a soft dough forms. On a lightly floured surface, use a floured rolling pin to roll out dough to ⅛-inch thickness. Transfer to an ungreased 9-inch deep-dish pie plate and use a sharp knife to trim edge of dough. Prick bottom of crust with a fork. Bake 5 minutes. Cool completely on a wire rack.

Reduce oven temperature to 375 degrees. For filling, melt butter in a large skillet over medium heat. Add green onions and garlic; cook until onions are tender. Add mushrooms;

Seasoned with garlic, basil, and thyme and loaded with Swiss cheese, Mushroom Pie makes a flavorful addition to your Christmas morning meal. Refreshingly different Minty Fruit Salad is tossed with a sweet mixture of honey and maraschino cherry juice.

cook until all liquid has evaporated. Remove from heat. Sprinkle half of cheese over crust. Spoon half of mushroom mixture over cheese. Repeat with remaining cheese and mushroom mixture.

In a medium bowl, whisk eggs, whipping cream, basil, thyme, salt, and pepper. Pour egg mixture into pie crust. Bake 40 to 45 minutes or until

a knife inserted in center of pie comes out clean. Let stand 10 minutes before serving. Serve warm or cool slightly, cover, and refrigerate.

To reheat, cover and bake in a preheated 350-degree oven 40 to 45 minutes or until heated through.

Yield: 8 to 10 servings

OVERNIGHT COFFEE CAKE

1 cup chopped pecans
3/4 cup firmly packed brown sugar
1 package (4 ounces) instant vanilla pudding mix
1 teaspoon ground cinnamon
1 package (25 ounces) frozen white yeast roll dough, thawed according to package directions
3/4 cup butter or margarine, melted

In a small bowl, combine pecans, brown sugar, pudding mix, and cinnamon. Sprinkle 3 tablespoons sugar mixture in bottom of a greased 10-inch tube pan. Dip each roll in melted butter and then in sugar mixture in bowl, covering each roll completely. Place a single layer of rolls with sides touching in pan. Sprinkle remaining sugar mixture over rolls. Pour remaining butter over rolls. Cover and refrigerate 8 hours or overnight.

Remove pan from refrigerator 30 minutes before baking, leave covered, and place in a warm place (80 to 85 degrees) to allow rolls to rise. Preheat oven to 350 degrees. Uncover and bake 40 to 45 minutes or until golden brown. (If top browns too quickly, cover with aluminum foil.) Cool in pan 15 minutes. Remove from pan and serve warm.
Yield: about 16 servings

Cool and creamy, Pineapple Frost is the perfect beverage to serve with breakfast. Overnight Coffee Cake is a tasty yet simple to fix treat. A pleasing combination of spinach, eggs, and cheeses baked atop croissant halves, Spinach-Feta Strata is sure to be a hit with holiday guests.

SPINACH-FETA STRATA

6 croissants, cut in half horizontally
6 eggs, beaten
1 1/2 cups milk
1 package (10 ounces) frozen chopped spinach, thawed and well drained
1/2 teaspoon salt
1/4 teaspoon ground black pepper
1/4 teaspoon ground nutmeg
1 1/2 cups (6 ounces) shredded Monterey Jack cheese
7 ounces crumbled feta cheese

Arrange croissant halves with sides overlapping in a greased 9 x 13-inch baking dish. In a medium bowl, combine eggs, milk, spinach, salt, pepper, and nutmeg. Pour over croissants. Sprinkle cheeses over spinach mixture. Cover and refrigerate 8 hours or overnight.

Preheat oven to 350 degrees. Uncover and bake 40 to 45 minutes or until lightly browned. Cut into squares. Serve warm.
Yield: about 15 servings

PINEAPPLE FROST

3 cups pineapple sherbet, softened
2 cans (8 ounces each) crushed pineapple, drained
2 cups half and half
2/3 cup light corn syrup
1 quart ginger ale, chilled

Process sherbet, pineapple, half and half, and corn syrup in a food processor until pineapple is very finely chopped. Pour into a medium metal or plastic bowl. Cover and freeze until firm.

Remove from freezer one hour before serving. To serve, place pineapple mixture in a 3-quart container; add ginger ale and stir to make a slush.
Yield: about 9 1/2 cups punch

SAUSAGE-GRITS PIE
(Shown on page 20)

CRUST
1 1/2 cups water
1/2 teaspoon garlic powder
1/2 cup quick-cooking grits
1/2 cup (2 ounces) shredded Cheddar cheese
1/4 cup all-purpose flour
1 egg, beaten

FILLING
6 eggs
1/2 teaspoon dry mustard
1/2 teaspoon salt
1/4 teaspoon ground black pepper
1/2 pound ground mild pork sausage, cooked, drained, and crumbled
1 cup (4 ounces) shredded Cheddar cheese
4 green onions, chopped

For crust, combine water and garlic powder in a medium saucepan. Bring to a boil. Stir in grits and bring to a boil again. Reduce heat to medium-low, cover, and cook 5 to 7 minutes or until thick, stirring occasionally. Remove from heat. In a small bowl, combine cheese, flour, and egg. Stir cheese mixture into grits. Press grits mixture into bottom and 2 inches up sides of a greased 9-inch springform pan.

Preheat oven to 350 degrees. For filling, whisk eggs, mustard, salt, and pepper in a large bowl. Stir in sausage, cheese, and onions. Pour into crust. Bake 45 to 50 minutes or until a knife inserted in center comes out clean. Serve hot or cool completely on a wire rack, cover, and refrigerate.

To reheat, cover and bake in a preheated 350-degree oven 30 to 35 minutes or until heated through. Remove sides of pan. Serve warm.
Yield: 8 to 10 servings

Featuring a savory cheese grits crust and a hearty filling of eggs, Cheddar cheese, sausage, and green onions, Sausage-Grits Pie (recipe on page 19) makes a delicious main dish.

SURPRISE MUFFINS

1/2 cup smooth peanut butter
1/2 cup semisweet chocolate chips
1 1/2 cups all-purpose flour
1 cup oat bran
1/2 cup firmly packed brown sugar
2 1/2 teaspoons baking powder
1/4 teaspoon salt
1 cup milk
1/3 cup vegetable oil
2 eggs
1 teaspoon maple extract

Preheat oven to 425 degrees. In a small bowl, combine peanut butter and chocolate chips; set aside.

In a medium bowl, combine flour, bran, brown sugar, baking powder, and salt. In a small bowl, whisk milk, oil, eggs, and maple extract. Make a well in center of dry ingredients and add milk mixture; stir just until moistened. Spoon about 2 tablespoons batter into each cup of a greased muffin pan. Spoon about 2 teaspoons peanut butter mixture over batter in each cup. Spoon remaining batter over peanut butter mixture, filling each cup three-fourths full. Bake 15 to 18 minutes or until muffins pull away from sides of pan. Remove from pan and cool completely on a wire rack. Store in an airtight container. Muffins may be served at room temperature or reheated.

To reheat, cover and bake in a preheated 350-degree oven 5 to 8 minutes or until heated through.
Yield: about 1 dozen muffins

A creamy chocolate-peanut butter filling is hidden in the center of these taste-tempting oat bran Surprise Muffins. Delectable pinwheel Praline Biscuits feature a luscious swirl of chopped pecans and brown sugar.

PRALINE BISCUITS

1 cup chopped pecans
1/4 cup firmly packed brown sugar
3 tablespoons butter or margarine, melted
1 teaspoon maple extract
2 cups all-purpose flour
2 teaspoons granulated sugar
1 teaspoon baking powder
1/2 teaspoon baking soda
1/4 teaspoon salt
1/2 cup vegetable shortening
3/4 cup milk

In a small bowl, combine pecans, brown sugar, butter, and maple extract; set aside.

In a medium bowl, combine flour, granulated sugar, baking powder, baking soda, and salt. Using a pastry blender or 2 knives, cut shortening into dry ingredients until mixture resembles coarse meal. Add milk, stirring just until moistened. Turn dough onto a lightly floured surface and knead about 2 minutes. Use a floured rolling pin to roll dough into

an 8 x 12-inch rectangle; spread pecan mixture over dough. Beginning at 1 long edge, roll up dough jellyroll style. Using a serrated knife, cut into twelve 1-inch-thick slices. Place slices with sides touching in a greased 7 x 11-inch baking dish. Cover and refrigerate until ready to bake.

Preheat oven to 400 degrees. Uncover biscuits and bake 22 to 25 minutes or until lightly browned. Serve warm.
Yield: 1 dozen biscuits

CHOCOLATE WAFFLES WITH CINNAMON-MARSHMALLOW TOPPING

WAFFLES

- 1/2 cup butter or margarine, softened
- 1 cup sugar
- 1/2 cup milk
- 2 eggs
- 1 teaspoon vanilla extract
- 1 1/2 cups sifted cake flour
- 2 teaspoons baking powder
- 1/4 teaspoon salt
- 2 ounces semisweet baking chocolate, melted

TOPPING

- 1 jar (7 ounces) marshmallow creme
- 2 tablespoons light corn syrup
- 1/2 teaspoon clear vanilla extract (used in cake decorating)
- 1/4 teaspoon ground cinnamon
  Shaved semisweet baking chocolate to garnish

For waffles, preheat waffle iron. In a large bowl, cream butter and sugar until fluffy. Add milk, eggs, and vanilla; beat until smooth. In a medium bowl, combine cake flour, baking powder, and salt. Add dry ingredients and melted chocolate to creamed mixture and blend (do not overmix). For each waffle, pour about 1/2 cup batter into waffle iron. Bake 5 to 7 minutes or according to manufacturer's instructions.

For topping, heat marshmallow creme and corn syrup over medium-low heat in a medium saucepan until marshmallow creme is smooth. Stir in vanilla and cinnamon. Serve waffles hot with warm topping. Garnish with shaved chocolate.

Yield: about six 7-inch waffles

Chocolate Waffles are a delightful alternative to typical morning fare. Drizzled with creamy Cinnamon-Marshmallow Topping, they can be a unique and elegant dessert, too!

22

Sweet Potato Biscuits stuffed with smoked ham taste great served hot from the oven. Hot Fruited Tea (recipe on page 25) is a warming drink your guests will welcome day or night.

SWEET POTATO BISCUITS

Fill these fragrant biscuits with smoked ham or turkey for a delicious treat.

1 sweet potato (10 -12 ounces), baked and peeled
1 1/2 cups sifted all-purpose flour
2 1/2 teaspoons baking powder
1/2 teaspoon salt
1/2 teaspoon ground cinnamon
1/2 teaspoon freshly grated nutmeg
1/4 teaspoon ground ginger
1/3 cup firmly packed dark brown sugar
1/2 cup unsalted butter, cut into pieces and softened
3 tablespoons whipping cream, divided
1 egg

Purée potato in a food processor or mash until smooth. Reserve 3/4 cup of potato and cool.

Position rack in upper third of oven. Preheat oven to 450 degrees. Sift flour, baking powder, salt, cinnamon, nutmeg, and ginger into a medium bowl. Stir in brown sugar. Using a pastry blender or 2 knives, cut butter into dry ingredients until mixture resembles coarse meal. Add reserved sweet potato and 2 tablespoons whipping cream; stir just until moistened. Turn onto a lightly floured surface and knead gently just until dough holds together. Use a floured rolling pin to roll out dough to 1/2-inch thickness, use a 2-inch biscuit cutter to cut out biscuits. Place biscuits on an ungreased baking sheet, spacing 1/2-inch apart. In a small bowl, combine egg and 1 tablespoon whipping cream. Brush tops with egg mixture. Bake 12 to 15 minutes or until golden brown. Cool 5 minutes before serving.

Yield: about 18 biscuits

23

HOT FRUITED TEA

(Shown on page 23)

This hot beverage will fill your home with a wonderful spicy aroma. After it is brewed, the tea may be refrigerated and reheated later. For larger crowds, we suggest serving the tea from an electric coffee server.

1 1/2 cups water
1/3 cup unsweetened powdered instant tea
1 can (46 ounces) pineapple juice
6 cups orange juice
6 cups lemonade
1 1/2 cups sugar
3 whole nutmegs
3 tablespoons whole cloves
4 2-inch cinnamon sticks
Sliced oranges or lemons to serve

In a large Dutch oven, bring water to a boil; stir in instant tea until dissolved. Stir in pineapple juice, orange juice, lemonade, and sugar, mixing well. Place nutmegs and cloves in center of a small square of cheesecloth and tie corners together to form a bag. Add spice bag and cinnamon sticks to tea. Stirring occasionally, simmer 2 to 3 hours over medium-low heat (do not allow mixture to boil). Remove spice bag and serve hot tea with slices of orange or lemon.
Yield: about 16 cups tea

APRICOT CONSERVE

1 package (6 ounces) dried apricots
1 cup sugar
1/2 cup slivered almonds, chopped
1/2 cup golden raisins
1/2 teaspoon ground cinnamon

Place apricots in a medium bowl. Add enough water to cover apricots. Cover bowl and allow to sit at room temperature overnight; drain.
In a large saucepan, combine apricots, sugar, almonds, raisins, and cinnamon. Stir over low heat until sugar dissolves. Stirring frequently, cook slowly until mixture thickens. Store in an airtight container in refrigerator.
Yield: about 2 cups conserve

HOT MAPLE CREAM

2 cups milk
2 cups half and half
1 teaspoon vanilla extract
1/2 cup maple syrup
1/8 teaspoon ground nutmeg
Freshly grated nutmeg to garnish

Combine milk, half and half, vanilla, maple syrup, and 1/8 teaspoon nutmeg in a heavy medium saucepan over medium-low heat. Stirring occasionally, heat mixture thoroughly (do not allow mixture to boil). Garnish with grated nutmeg. Serve warm.
Yield: about 4 1/2 cups punch

LIGHT YEAST BISCUITS

1 package dry yeast
2 tablespoons warm water
2 tablespoons sugar, divided
2 1/2 cups all-purpose flour
1/2 teaspoon baking powder
1/2 teaspoon baking soda
1/2 teaspoon salt
1/2 cup butter or margarine, softened
1 cup buttermilk, warmed
Vegetable cooking spray

In a small bowl, dissolve yeast in warm water; stir in 1 tablespoon sugar. In a large bowl, combine remaining 1 tablespoon sugar, flour, baking powder, baking soda, and salt. Using a pastry blender or two knives, cut butter into dry ingredients until mixture resembles coarse cornmeal. Add buttermilk and yeast mixture to dry ingredients; stir until a soft dough forms. Turn onto a lightly floured surface and knead 4 minutes or until dough becomes smooth and elastic. Place in a large bowl sprayed with cooking spray, turning once to coat top of dough. Cover and let rise in a warm place (80 to 85 degrees) 1 to 1 1/2 hours or until doubled in size.
Turn dough onto a lightly floured surface and punch down. Use a floured rolling pin to roll out dough to 1/2-inch thickness. Use a 2-inch-diameter biscuit cutter to cut out biscuits. Place biscuits 1 inch apart on an ungreased baking sheet. Spray tops with cooking spray, cover, and let rise in a warm place 30 to 45 minutes or until doubled in size.
Preheat oven to 400 degrees. Bake 12 to 15 minutes or until golden brown. Serve warm.
Yield: about 2 dozen biscuits

For tasty help-yourself tidbits, set out a basket of buttery Light Yeast Biscuits along with our nutty, fruity Apricot Conserve (not shown). A dash of nutmeg adds spice to Hot Maple Cream, a flavorful winter warmer.

25

Tossed with a luscious blend of honey, ginger, and orange juice, Gingered Fruit Salad is pleasingly different.

GINGERED FRUIT SALAD

Gingered Fruit Salad may be made one day in advance.

1 can (20 ounces) pineapple chunks, drained
1 package (16 ounces) frozen unsweetened peach slices, thawed
1 cup coarsely chopped fresh pear (about 1 medium pear)
1 cup coarsely chopped apple (about 1 medium apple)
1/4 cup honey
2 tablespoons orange juice concentrate, thawed
2 teaspoons ground ginger

In a large bowl, combine pineapple chunks, peach slices, pear, and apple. In a small bowl, combine honey, orange juice, and ginger. Pour over fruit; toss until well coated. Cover and refrigerate 8 hours or overnight. Serve chilled.

Yield: about 8 servings

OVEN-BAKED FRENCH TOAST

8 1/2-inch-thick slices French bread (about half of a 1-pound loaf)
1/2 cup raisins
1/2 cup chopped pecans
2 cups half and half
6 eggs
1/2 cup orange-flavored liqueur
1 teaspoon ground cinnamon
1/2 teaspoon salt
1/4 teaspoon ground nutmeg
   Sifted confectioners sugar or Orange Syrup (recipe on this page) to serve

Arrange bread slices in a single layer with sides touching in a greased 10 1/2 x 15 1/2-inch jellyroll pan. Sprinkle raisins and pecans over bread. In a medium bowl, whisk half and half, eggs, liqueur, cinnamon, salt, and nutmeg. Pour egg mixture over bread. Cover and refrigerate 8 hours or overnight.

Preheat oven to 400 degrees. Uncover and bake French toast 30 to 35 minutes or until a toothpick inserted in center comes out clean and toast is lightly browned. To serve, dust with confectioners sugar or pour warm Orange Syrup over slices of toast.
Yield: 8 servings

ORANGE SYRUP

1 bottle (12 ounces) pancake syrup
1 teaspoon orange extract

In a small saucepan, heat syrup until hot. Remove from heat; stir in orange extract. Serve warm with Oven-Baked French Toast.
Yield: about 1 1/2 cups syrup

Flavored with cinnamon, nutmeg, and orange liqueur, Oven-Baked French Toast is sprinkled with raisins and pecans for a delightful treat. Warm Orange Syrup makes a yummy topping.

Baked Spiced Fruit is a warm compote of spiced apples, peaches, pineapple, and cherries cooked in a cinnamony brown sugar sauce. Your guests can take a Christmas coffee break with hearty Banana-Raisin Bran Muffins.

BAKED SPICED FRUIT

1   can (29 ounces) peach halves
      in heavy syrup, drained
1   can (20 ounces) pineapple
      slices in fruit juice, drained,
      reserving 3/4 cup of juice
1   jar (about 14 ounces) spiced
      apple rings, drained
1/2 cup drained maraschino cherries
3/4 cup firmly packed brown sugar
1/3 cup butter or margarine
1   teaspoon ground cinnamon
1/4 teaspoon ground cloves
1/4 teaspoon curry powder
4   teaspoons cornstarch
4   teaspoons water

Preheat oven to 350 degrees. Arrange peaches, pineapple slices, apple rings, and maraschino cherries in a 9 x 13-inch baking dish. In a small saucepan over medium heat, combine reserved pineapple juice, brown sugar, butter, cinnamon, cloves, and curry powder. In a small bowl, dissolve cornstarch in water. Stirring pineapple juice mixture frequently, cook 7 to 8 minutes. Stirring constantly, add cornstarch mixture and continue to cook about 2 minutes or until mixture thickens. Pour sauce over fruit. Bake 25 to 30 minutes or until bubbly. Serve warm.
Yield: about 14 servings

BANANA-RAISIN BRAN MUFFINS

1   cup all-purpose flour
3/4 cup whole-wheat flour
1/3 cup sugar
2   teaspoons baking powder
1/2 teaspoon baking soda
1/2 teaspoon salt
2   eggs
1/2 cup buttermilk
1/2 cup vegetable oil
2   medium bananas, mashed
2   cups raisin bran flakes

Preheat oven to 350 degrees. In a medium bowl, combine flours, sugar, baking powder, baking soda, and salt. In a small bowl, whisk eggs, buttermilk, oil, and bananas. Add buttermilk mixture and raisin bran flakes to dry ingredients; stir until ingredients are moistened. Fill paper-lined muffin cups two-thirds full. Bake 25 to 30 minutes or until golden brown. Serve warm.
Yield: about 18 muffins

The rich flavors of ginger and molasses in the batter make these Gingerbread Pancakes a perfect addition to a holiday brunch.

GINGERBREAD PANCAKES

1 1/2 cups all-purpose flour
1/4 cup sugar
1 teaspoon ground ginger
1 teaspoon baking powder
1 teaspoon baking soda
1/2 teaspoon salt
1 cup buttermilk
3 eggs, beaten
1/3 cup butter or margarine, melted
1/4 cup molasses
Butter or margarine
Butter and syrup to serve

In a large bowl, combine flour, sugar, ginger, baking powder, baking soda, and salt. In a medium bowl, whisk buttermilk, eggs, 1/3 cup melted butter, and molasses. Add to dry ingredients and stir just until blended.

Melt 2 tablespoons butter in a large skillet over medium heat. For each pancake, pour about 1/4 cup batter into skillet and cook until pancake is full of bubbles on top and underside is lightly browned. Turn with a spatula and cook until other side is lightly browned. Transfer to a warm plate, cover with aluminum foil, and place in a 200-degree oven until ready to serve. Add butter to skillet as necessary between batches. Serve hot with butter and syrup.
Yield: about 1 1/2 dozen pancakes

FETA CHEESE-VEGETABLE SALAD

DRESSING

- 1 cup chopped fresh basil leaves **or** 2 tablespoons dried basil leaves, crushed
- 3/4 cup balsamic vinegar
- 2/3 cup buttermilk
- 1/3 cup olive oil
- 1 tablespoon Dijon-style mustard
- 2 teaspoons salt
- 1 teaspoon ground black pepper
- 1/2 teaspoon garlic powder

SALAD

- 3 cups fresh broccoli flowerets
- 3 cups shredded green cabbage
- 2 cups thinly sliced zucchini
- 1 1/2 cups sliced red onions
- 1 1/2 cups thinly sliced carrots
- 1 1/2 cups (10 ounces) crumbled feta cheese

For dressing, combine basil, vinegar, buttermilk, oil, mustard, salt, pepper, and garlic powder in a 1-pint jar with a tight-fitting lid. Shake until well blended. Refrigerate 8 hours or overnight to allow flavors to blend.

In a large bowl, combine broccoli, cabbage, zucchini, onions, and carrots. Pour dressing over vegetables; stir until well coated. Stir in cheese.

Yield: about 12 cups salad

CAVIAR MOUSSE

- 1 teaspoon unflavored gelatin
- 2 tablespoons cold water
- 2 tablespoons boiling water
- 2 tablespoons mayonnaise
- 1/2 tablespoon finely chopped fresh dill weed **or** 1/2 teaspoon dried dill weed
- 1 teaspoon lemon juice
- 1 teaspoon finely chopped onion
- 1/4 teaspoon hot pepper sauce
- 1/4 teaspoon paprika
- 1 jar (2 ounces) red lumpfish caviar, well drained
- 1/4 cup whipping cream
- 2 large cucumbers
  Fresh dill weed to garnish

Caviar Mousse is served atop cucumber slices for an elegant appetizer. Feta Cheese-Vegetable Salad features crisp fresh vegetables with a tangy buttermilk-and-basil dressing.

Place a medium bowl and beaters from an electric mixer in freezer. In another medium bowl, combine gelatin and cold water; allow to stand 1 minute. Add boiling water and stir until gelatin dissolves. Cool to room temperature. Whisk in mayonnaise, dill weed, lemon juice, onion, pepper sauce, and paprika. Cover and refrigerate 5 minutes or until slightly thickened. Fold caviar into gelatin mixture.

In chilled bowl, beat whipping cream until stiff peaks form. Fold whipped cream into caviar mixture. Cover and chill 2 hours or until set. Reserving 1/4 of 1 cucumber, slice remaining cucumbers into 1/4-inch-thick slices. Spoon rounded teaspoonfuls of caviar mixture onto cucumber slices. Cut reserved 1/4 cucumber into 1/8-inch-thick slices and then into quarters. Garnish each appetizer with a cucumber quarter and dill weed.

Yield: about 1 1/2 dozen appetizers

CHICKEN-CUCUMBER SALAD

1½ pounds boneless, skinless
    chicken breasts
1 package (8 ounces) cream
    cheese, softened
½ cup sour cream
2 tablespoons dry white wine
1½ teaspoons garlic powder
1 teaspoon salt
½ teaspoon ground black pepper
½ teaspoon dried dill weed
½ teaspoon hot pepper sauce
1 cup peeled, diced cucumber
½ cup chopped green onions
4 acorn squash, halved
    lengthwise and seeded
    Fresh carrot and green pepper
    slices to garnish

In a medium saucepan, cover chicken with water. Bring to a boil, reduce heat to medium-low, and simmer 30 to 35 minutes or until chicken is cooked; drain. Cool 10 minutes and cut into bite-size pieces.

In a medium bowl, beat cream cheese and sour cream until fluffy. Beat in wine, garlic powder, salt, pepper, dill weed, and pepper sauce. Stir in chicken, cucumber, and green onions. Cut a thin slice off bottom of each squash half so squash will sit level. Spoon chicken salad into each squash half. Refer to photo and garnish with carrot and green pepper slices. Cover and refrigerate until ready to serve.
Yield: 8 servings

HOT BERRY-BRANDY PUNCH

2 packages (12 ounces each)
    frozen red raspberries,
    thawed
1 gallon cranberry juice cocktail
2 cups sugar
2 cups blackberry-flavored brandy
½ cup raspberry-flavored liqueur

Cool, creamy Chicken-Cucumber Salad is attractively presented in acorn squash halves. Hot Berry-Brandy Punch is deliciously fruity.

Purée raspberries in a food processor. Strain raspberries; discard seeds and pulp. In a Dutch oven, combine raspberry purée, cranberry juice, sugar, brandy, and liqueur.

Bring to a boil; stir until sugar dissolves. Serve warm.
Yield: about 19½ cups punch

Chocolate Bread Pudding is an old-fashioned favorite with a chocolate twist! A drizzling of warm Caramel Sauce makes the moist dessert irresistible.

CHOCOLATE BREAD PUDDING WITH CARAMEL SAUCE

BREAD PUDDING
- 1 can (10 biscuits) refrigerated buttermilk biscuits, baked according to package directions
- 2 cups milk
- 2 eggs
- 2 tablespoons butter or margarine, melted
- 2 teaspoons vanilla extract
- 3/4 cup sugar
- 1/4 cup cocoa
- 1/2 cup semisweet chocolate chips

CARAMEL SAUCE
- 1/2 cup butter or margarine
- 1/2 cup firmly packed brown sugar
- 1/2 cup granulated sugar
- 1/2 cup evaporated milk
- 1 tablespoon vanilla extract

Preheat oven to 350 degrees. For bread pudding, tear baked biscuits into bite-size pieces. In a large bowl, combine biscuits and milk; set aside. In a medium bowl, beat eggs, melted butter, and vanilla until well blended. Add sugar and cocoa; beat until well blended. Stir in chocolate chips. Add chocolate mixture to biscuit mixture; stir until well blended. Pour into a greased 8-inch square glass baking dish. Bake 55 to 60 minutes or until set in center and edges pull away from sides of pan.

For caramel sauce, combine butter, sugars, and milk in a medium saucepan. Stirring constantly, cook over low heat until butter melts and sugars dissolve. Increase heat to medium and bring to a boil. Stirring constantly, boil about 9 minutes or until thickened. Remove from heat; stir in vanilla. Cut warm bread pudding into squares and serve with warm sauce.

Yield: about 9 servings

This delicious Caramel-Nut Spice Cake tastes like it came from the bakery, but it's amazingly simple to make! The rich cake is crowned with a warm caramel glaze and a sprinkling of nuts.

CARAMEL-NUT SPICE CAKE

1 package (18.25 ounces) spice cake mix
1 package (3.5 ounces) butterscotch instant pudding mix
4 eggs
1¼ cups water
½ cup vegetable oil
24 caramels (about ½ of a 14-ounce package)
3 tablespoons water
¼ cup chopped walnuts

Preheat oven to 350 degrees. Combine cake mix, pudding mix, eggs, 1¼ cups water, and oil in a large bowl; beat until well blended. Pour into a greased 10-inch fluted tube pan. Bake 43 to 47 minutes or until a toothpick inserted in center of cake comes out clean. Allow cake to cool in pan on a wire rack 20 minutes. Invert cake onto a serving plate.

In a medium microwave-safe bowl, combine caramels and 3 tablespoons water. Microwave on medium-high power (80%) 3 minutes or until caramels melt, stirring after each minute. Stir in walnuts. Drizzle caramel mixture over warm cake. Allow cake to cool completely. Store in an airtight container.
Yield: about 16 servings

SANTA'S SWEETSHOP

*T*he very thought of Christmas inspires visions of Santa's sweetshop for children of all ages. With the magical treats in this section, you can transform your kitchen into a delicious wonderland of sweets. Our offerings include a fanciful variety of surprises — from moist, chewy cookies to creamy fudge and tempting candies — that will please every member of the family.

The heartwarming taste of home-baked gingerbread is always a holiday favorite. This year, share the goodness with these Gingerbread House Cookies (recipe on page 36).

GINGERBREAD HOUSE COOKIES

(Shown on pages 34 and 35)

COOKIES

- 1/2 cup butter or margarine, softened
- 1/2 cup firmly packed brown sugar
- 1/2 cup molasses
- 1 egg
- 2 1/2 cups all-purpose flour
- 2 teaspoons ground ginger
- 1 teaspoon ground cinnamon
- 1 teaspoon baking soda
- 1/2 teaspoon ground nutmeg
- 1/4 teaspoon ground cloves
- 1/4 teaspoon salt

ROYAL ICING

- 2 2/3 cups sifted confectioners sugar
- 4 tablespoons warm water
- 2 tablespoons meringue powder
- 1/2 teaspoon lemon extract
  Candies, mints, and gumdrops to decorate

Preheat oven to 350 degrees. For cookies, cream butter and brown sugar in a large bowl until fluffy. Add molasses and egg; beat until smooth. In a medium bowl, combine flour, ginger, cinnamon, baking soda, nutmeg, cloves, and salt. Add dry ingredients to creamed mixture; stir until a soft dough forms. On a lightly floured surface, use a floured rolling pin to roll out dough to 1/4-inch thickness. Use a floured 5 x 7 1/2-inch gingerbread house-shaped cookie cutter to cut out cookies. Transfer to a greased baking sheet. Bake 10 to 12 minutes or until edges are firm. Transfer cookies to a wire rack with waxed paper underneath to cool completely.

For royal icing, beat confectioners sugar, water, meringue powder, and lemon extract in a medium bowl with an electric mixer 7 to 10 minutes or until stiff. Spoon icing into a pastry bag fitted with a medium round tip. Pipe icing onto cookies. Use candies, mints, and gumdrops to decorate

cookies as desired. Allow icing to harden. Store in an airtight container.
Yield: 6 cookies

WALNUT BUTTER COOKIES

- 1 cup chopped walnuts
- 2 cups all-purpose flour
- 1/4 teaspoon baking soda
- 1/8 teaspoon salt
- 1 cup chilled butter or margarine
- 1/2 cup granulated sugar
- 1 egg yolk
- 2 1/2 teaspoons vanilla extract
  Sifted confectioners sugar

Preheat oven to 350 degrees. To toast walnuts, spread evenly on an ungreased baking sheet. Stirring occasionally, bake 5 to 8 minutes or until darker in color. Cool completely on baking sheet. Process walnuts in a food processor until finely ground.

In a large bowl, combine flour, baking soda, and salt. Using a pastry blender or 2 knives, cut butter into flour mixture until mixture resembles coarse meal. Add ground walnuts, granulated sugar, egg yolk, and vanilla; stir until a soft dough forms. Shape dough into 1-inch balls and place 2 inches apart on a greased baking sheet. Press balls with back of a fork in a crisscross pattern to form 1/4-inch-thick cookies. Bake 15 to 20 minutes or until edges are lightly browned. Transfer cookies to a wire rack with waxed paper underneath. Dust warm cookies with confectioners sugar; cool completely. Dust with confectioners sugar again. Store in an airtight container.
Yield: about 5 dozen cookies

DRIED FRUIT TRUFFLES

- 3/4 cup whipping cream
- 6 tablespoons butter or margarine
- 3 tablespoons corn syrup
- 1 package (12 ounces) semisweet chocolate chips
- 2/3 cup finely chopped pitted prunes
- 2/3 cup finely chopped walnuts
- 1 tablespoon cognac
  Cocoa

In a medium saucepan, combine whipping cream, butter, and corn syrup. Stirring constantly, cook over medium heat until mixture begins to boil. Remove from heat; add chocolate chips and stir until smooth. Stir in prunes, walnuts, and cognac. Pour into a greased 8-inch square baking pan. Cover and refrigerate 8 hours or until firm enough to handle.

Cut into 1-inch squares. Shape each square into a ball and roll in cocoa. Place balls in petit-four cups. Cover and chill about 4 hours or until firm. Store in refrigerator.
Yield: about 5 dozen truffles

A dusting of confectioners sugar gives crispy Walnut Butter Cookies a snowy look. Flavored with cognac and dark chocolate, our Dried Fruit Truffles are rich and delicious.

PEANUT BUTTER DIVINITY

2 cups sugar
1/2 cup light corn syrup
1/2 cup water
1/8 teaspoon salt
2 egg whites
1 teaspoon vanilla extract
1 cup crunchy peanut butter

Butter sides of a large saucepan or Dutch oven. Combine sugar, corn syrup, water, and salt in saucepan. Stirring constantly, cook over medium-low heat until sugar dissolves. Using a pastry brush dipped in hot water, wash down any sugar crystals on sides of pan. Attach a candy thermometer to pan, making sure thermometer does not touch bottom of pan. Increase heat to medium and bring to a boil.

While syrup mixture is boiling, use highest speed of an electric mixer to beat egg whites in a large bowl until stiff peaks form; set aside.

Cook syrup mixture, without stirring, until mixture reaches firm-ball stage (approximately 242 to 248 degrees). Test about 1/2 teaspoon mixture in ice water. Mixture will roll into a firm ball in ice water but will flatten if pressed when removed from the water. While beating egg whites at low speed, slowly pour hot mixture into egg whites. Add vanilla and increase speed of mixer to high. Continue to beat until candy is no longer glossy. Fold in peanut butter. Pour into a buttered 8-inch square baking dish. Allow to harden. Cut into 1-inch squares. Store in an airtight container in refrigerator.
Yield: about 5 dozen squares divinity

PECAN LACE COOKIES

1 cup finely chopped pecans
1/2 cup butter or margarine, softened
1/2 cup firmly packed brown sugar
2 tablespoons rum, divided
2 tablespoons whipping cream
1/3 cup semisweet chocolate chips

Our Peanut Butter Divinity is a delicious variation of a favorite holiday candy. Light and delicate, Pecan Lace Cookies have a chocolaty flavor.

1/4 cup all-purpose flour
1/4 teaspoon salt
1/8 teaspoon baking soda
1 cup quick-cooking oats

Preheat oven to 350 degrees. To toast pecans, spread evenly on an ungreased baking sheet. Stirring occasionally, bake 5 to 8 minutes or until darker in color. Cool completely on baking sheet.

In a large bowl, cream butter and brown sugar until fluffy. Beat in 1 tablespoon rum. In a small saucepan, bring whipping cream to a boil over medium heat. Reduce heat to medium-low. Stir in remaining 1 tablespoon rum and simmer 2 to 3 minutes. Remove from heat; add chocolate chips and stir until smooth. Add chocolate mixture to creamed mixture and stir until well blended. Sift flour, salt, and baking soda into a medium bowl. Stir dry ingredients into chocolate mixture. Fold in oats and toasted pecans. Drop heaping teaspoonfuls of dough 4 inches apart onto a greased baking sheet. Use fingers to press each cookie into a 2-inch-diameter circle. Bake 8 minutes (cookies will be soft); cool on baking sheet 3 minutes. Transfer cookies to a wire rack to cool completely. Store in an airtight container.
Yield: about 4 dozen cookies

Fudgy Peanut Butter Bites are irresistible to candy lovers! Featuring a center of crunchy peanut butter, the fudge is incredibly rich and creamy.

FUDGY PEANUT BUTTER BITES

4 cups sugar
1 cup evaporated milk
1/3 cup corn syrup
6 tablespoons butter or margarine
2 tablespoons honey
1/2 teaspoon vanilla extract
1 package (6 ounces) semisweet chocolate chips
1 1/2 cups crunchy peanut butter

Butter sides of a large saucepan or Dutch oven. Combine sugar, evaporated milk, corn syrup, butter, and honey in saucepan. Stirring constantly, cook over medium-low heat until sugar dissolves. Using a pastry brush dipped in hot water, wash down any sugar crystals on sides of pan. Attach a candy thermometer to pan, making sure thermometer does not touch bottom of pan. Increase heat to medium and bring to a boil. Cook, without stirring, until mixture reaches soft-ball stage (approximately 234 to 240 degrees). Test about 1/2 teaspoon mixture in ice water. Mixture will easily form a ball in ice water but flatten when held in your hand. Place pan in 2 inches of cold water in sink. Add vanilla; do not stir until mixture cools to approximately 120 degrees. Stir in chocolate chips.

Using medium speed of an electric mixer, beat fudge until thickened and no longer glossy. Divide fudge in half. Place each half on a separate piece (22 inches long) of plastic wrap. Use a greased rolling pin to roll each half of fudge into a 5 x 18-inch rectangle. Spread 3/4 cup peanut butter lengthwise along center of each rectangle. Fold long edges of each rectangle over peanut butter to form an 18-inch-long roll; pinch edges to seal. Wrap in plastic wrap and refrigerate until firm. Cut into 1/2-inch slices. Store in an airtight container in refrigerator.
Yield: about 6 dozen pieces fudge

BAKED BANANA SQUARES

CRUST
1¼ cups graham cracker crumbs
¼ cup sugar
¼ cup butter or margarine, melted

TOPPING
¼ cup butter or margarine
4 firm bananas, cut into ½-inch
   slices
1 tablespoon freshly squeezed
   lemon juice
1 teaspoon dried lemon peel
¼ cup firmly packed brown sugar

Preheat oven to 375 degrees.
For crust, combine cracker crumbs,
sugar, and melted butter in a
medium bowl; stir until well blended.
Press into bottom of a greased
8-inch square baking dish. Bake
5 to 6 minutes or until browned.
For topping, melt butter in a
medium saucepan over low heat.
Add bananas, lemon juice, and
lemon peel; stir until bananas are well
coated. Arrange banana slices on
crust. Sprinkle brown sugar over
bananas and bake 12 to 15 minutes
or until bubbly. Cut into 2-inch
squares. Serve warm.
Yield: about 16 squares

MIXED NUT BRITTLE

1½ cups sugar
½ cup light corn syrup
¼ cup water
1½ tablespoons butter or margarine
½ teaspoon salt
¾ cup lightly salted mixed nuts
1 teaspoon baking soda

Butter sides of a 3-quart heavy
saucepan. Combine sugar, corn
syrup, and water in saucepan. Stirring
constantly, cook over medium-low
heat until sugar dissolves. Using a
pastry brush dipped in hot water,
wash down any sugar crystals on
sides of pan. Attach a candy
thermometer to pan, making sure

Nestled on a graham cracker crust, Baked Banana Squares are sprinkled with brown sugar and served warm for a yummy treat.

thermometer does not touch bottom of
pan. Increase heat to medium and
bring to a boil. Cook, without stirring,
until mixture reaches hard-crack stage
(approximately 300 to 310 degrees)
and turns light golden in color. Test
about ½ teaspoon mixture in ice
water. Mixture should form brittle
threads in ice water and remain brittle
when removed from the water. Remove
mixture from heat and add butter and
salt; stir until butter melts. Add nuts
and baking soda (syrup will foam);
stir until baking soda dissolves.
Pour candy into a buttered
10½ x 15½-inch jellyroll pan.
Using a buttered spatula, spread
candy to edges of pan. Allow to cool
completely. Break into pieces. Store
in an airtight container.
Yield: about 1½ pounds brittle

Mixed nuts make a traditional candy extra fancy in Mixed Nut Brittle. Cut in a wreath shape, Lemon-Iced Apple Cookies are decorated with icing leaves and gold dragées.

LEMON-ICED APPLE COOKIES

COOKIES
- 1 cup butter or margarine, softened
- ³/₄ cup sugar
- ¹/₂ cup apple jelly
- 1 teaspoon vanilla extract
- 3 cups all-purpose flour

ICING
- 4¹/₂ cups sifted confectioners sugar
- ³/₄ cup milk
- 1 teaspoon lemon extract
  Gold dragées and purchased green decorating icing and set of decorating tips to decorate

For cookies, cream butter and sugar in a large bowl until fluffy. Add jelly and vanilla; beat until well blended. Add flour; stir until a soft dough forms. Cover and chill 30 minutes.

Preheat oven to 300 degrees. On a lightly floured surface, use a floured rolling pin to roll out dough to ¹/₄-inch thickness. Use a 3-inch-wide wreath-shaped cookie cutter to cut out cookies. Transfer to a greased baking sheet. Bake 20 to 25 minutes or until cookies are lightly browned. Transfer cookies to a wire rack to cool completely.

For icing, combine confectioners sugar, milk, and lemon extract in a large bowl; stir until smooth. Ice cookies. Decorate with dragées. Allow icing to harden. Use green decorating icing fitted with a leaf tip to pipe leaves onto cookies. Decorate leaves with dragées. Allow icing to harden. Store in an airtight container.
Yield: about 4 dozen cookies

Chocolate and ginger make Gingerbread Brownies an extra-special treat. Triple Chip Cookies are made with three kinds of baking chips and a surprise ingredient — crunchy granola cereal.

TRIPLE CHIP COOKIES

¹/₂ cup butter or margarine,
    softened
¹/₄ cup granulated sugar
¹/₄ cup firmly packed brown sugar
1 egg
¹/₂ teaspoon vanilla extract
1¹/₄ cups all-purpose flour
¹/₂ teaspoon baking soda
¹/₄ teaspoon salt
¹/₂ cup plain granola cereal
    (without fruit and nuts)

¹/₃ cup semisweet chocolate chips
¹/₃ cup milk chocolate chips
¹/₃ cup vanilla baking chips

Preheat oven to 375 degrees. In a large bowl, cream butter and sugars until fluffy. Add egg and vanilla; beat until smooth. Sift flour, baking soda, and salt into a small bowl. Stir in cereal. Add dry ingredients to

creamed mixture; stir until a soft dough forms. Fold in chips. Drop heaping teaspoonfuls of dough 2 inches apart onto a greased baking sheet. Bake 8 to 10 minutes or until edges are brown. Transfer cookies to a wire rack to cool completely. Store in an airtight container.
Yield: about 3¹/₂ dozen cookies

GINGERBREAD BROWNIES

BROWNIES
- 1/2 cup butter or margarine, softened
- 1 cup sugar
- 2 eggs
- 1 package (6 ounces) semisweet chocolate chips, melted
- 3/4 cup hot water
- 3/4 cup molasses
- 2 1/2 cups all-purpose flour
- 2 teaspoons ground ginger
- 2 teaspoons baking soda
- 1/2 teaspoon salt
- 1 cup finely chopped walnuts

ICING
- 1 cup sifted confectioners sugar
- 4 tablespoons milk

Preheat oven to 350 degrees. For brownies, cream butter and sugar in a large bowl until fluffy. Add eggs; beat until smooth. Add chocolate chips, water, and molasses; stir until well blended. Sift flour, ginger, baking soda, and salt into a medium bowl. Add dry ingredients to creamed mixture; stir until well blended. Stir in walnuts. Pour batter into a greased 10 1/2 x 15 1/2-inch jellyroll pan. Bake 30 to 35 minutes or until a toothpick inserted in center of brownies comes out clean. Cool in pan on a wire rack.

For icing, combine confectioners sugar and milk in a medium bowl; stir until smooth. Ice brownies. Allow icing to harden. Cut into 2-inch squares. Store in an airtight container.
Yield: about 3 dozen brownies

CINNAMON-CHOCOLATE STARS

Use icing on cookies to be eaten and gold petal dust on cookies to be used for decoration.

COOKIES
- 1 cup butter or margarine, softened
- 3/4 cup sugar
- 1 egg

Iced Cinnamon-Chocolate Stars will bring heavenly flavor to the holidays. The crisp shortbread cookies can also be brushed with gold and used as decorations.

- 1 teaspoon vanilla extract
- 1 package (6 ounces) semisweet chocolate chips, melted
- 3 cups all-purpose flour
- 1/2 teaspoon ground cinnamon
- 1/4 teaspoon salt

ICING
- 1 cup plus 2 tablespoons sifted confectioners sugar
- 3 tablespoons milk
  Gold petal dust (available at gourmet food stores) to decorate

Preheat oven to 300 degrees. For cookies, cream butter and sugar in a large bowl until fluffy. Add egg and vanilla; beat until smooth. Stir in chocolate chips. Sift flour, cinnamon, and salt into a medium bowl. Add dry ingredients to chocolate mixture; knead until a soft dough forms. On a lightly floured surface, use a floured rolling pin to roll out dough to 1/4-inch thickness. Use 1 1/2- to 2 1/2-inch star-shaped cookie cutters to cut out cookies. Transfer to a greased baking sheet. Bake 15 to 20 minutes or until firm. Transfer cookies to a wire rack to cool completely.

For icing, combine sugar and milk in a medium bowl until smooth. Ice cookies to be eaten; allow icing to harden.

For decorated cookies, use a small paintbrush to lightly apply petal dust to cookies. Store in an airtight container.
Yield: about 7 dozen cookies

APPLE-CINNAMON COOKIES

- 1 can (21 ounces) apple pie filling
- 1/2 cup butter or margarine, softened
- 1/2 cup granulated sugar, divided
- 1/4 cup firmly packed brown sugar
- 1 egg
- 1/2 teaspoon vanilla extract
- 1 1/2 cups all-purpose flour
- 1 teaspoon ground cinnamon, divided
- 1/2 teaspoon baking soda
- 1/2 teaspoon salt
- 3/4 cup finely chopped walnuts

Preheat oven to 375 degrees. Using a slotted spoon, remove 1 cup apples from pie filling. Set aside remaining pie filling for another use. Process apples in a food processor until finely chopped. In a large bowl, cream butter, 1/4 cup granulated sugar, and brown sugar until fluffy. Add egg and vanilla; beat until smooth. Add chopped apples to creamed mixture; stir until well blended. Sift flour, 1/2 teaspoon cinnamon, baking soda, and salt into a medium bowl. Add dry ingredients to creamed mixture; stir until a soft dough forms. Fold in walnuts. In a small bowl, combine remaining 1/4 cup granulated sugar and 1/2 teaspoon cinnamon; stir until well blended. Drop heaping teaspoonfuls of dough 2 inches apart onto a greased baking sheet. Sprinkle with sugar mixture. Bake 10 to 12 minutes or until edges are lightly browned. Transfer cookies to a wire rack to cool completely. Store in an airtight container.
Yield: about 3 1/2 dozen cookies

With their old-fashioned taste, these goodies are sure to become family favorites. Chopped walnuts make moist, cake-like Apple-Cinnamon Cookies especially nice. The chewy Orange Nut Squares are topped with cinnamon icing.

ORANGE NUT SQUARES

- 2 cups old-fashioned oats
- 1 cup all-purpose flour
- 3/4 cup firmly packed brown sugar
- 1 1/4 teaspoons ground cinnamon, divided
- 1/2 teaspoon baking soda
- 3/4 cup butter or margarine, melted
- 1 cup raisins
- 1/2 cup finely chopped walnuts
- 1/4 cup orange marmalade
- 1/2 cup sifted confectioners sugar
- 1 tablespoon milk

Preheat oven to 350 degrees. In a large bowl, combine oats, flour, brown sugar, 1 teaspoon cinnamon, and baking soda. Stir in melted butter until well blended. Reserving 1 cup oat mixture, press remaining oat mixture into bottom of a greased 8 x 11-inch baking pan. In a medium bowl, combine reserved oat mixture, raisins, walnuts, and marmalade. Spread raisin mixture evenly over oat mixture in pan. Bake 25 to 30 minutes or until lightly browned. While still warm, cut into 1-inch squares. In a small bowl, combine confectioners sugar, remaining 1/4 teaspoon cinnamon, and milk; stir until smooth. Drizzle over warm squares; cool completely in pan. Store in an airtight container.

Yield: about 4 dozen squares

Teatime Snowcaps are sweet bar cookies with a pastry crust and a topping of apricot jam, meringue, coconut, and sliced almonds.

TEATIME SNOWCAPS

CRUST
- 3/4 cup vegetable shortening
- 3/4 cup sifted confectioners sugar
- 1 1/2 cups all-purpose flour

TOPPING
- 1 1/4 cups apricot jam
- 3 egg whites
- 3/4 cup sugar
- 3/4 cup coconut, divided
- 1 cup sliced almonds, divided

Preheat oven to 350 degrees. For crust, cream shortening and confectioners sugar in a medium bowl. Stir in flour. Press mixture evenly into bottom of an ungreased 9 x 13-inch baking pan. Bake 12 to 15 minutes or until crust is lightly browned.

For topping, spread jam over hot crust. Beat egg whites until soft peaks form. Gradually beat in sugar, a few tablespoons at a time, until mixture is stiff and glossy. Fold in 1/2 cup coconut and 1/2 cup almonds. Spread mixture over jam. Sprinkle remaining coconut and almonds over top. Bake 20 minutes. Allow to cool. Cut into squares. Store in an airtight container.

Yield: about 35 cookies

After an afternoon of sledding or building snowmen, you'll be glad to come inside to these treats! Chewy Cashew-Fudge Tarts are brownie-like treats nestled in flaky pastry shells. Lightly sweet Cardamom Shortbread can be baked in a shortbread mold for a lovely embossed effect.

CARDAMOM SHORTBREAD

1/2	cup butter or margarine, softened
1/4	cup sugar
1	cup quick-cooking oats
1	teaspoon vanilla extract
2/3	cup all-purpose flour
1	teaspoon ground cardamom

Preheat oven to 350 degrees. In a medium bowl, cream butter and sugar until fluffy. Stir in oats and vanilla. Sift flour and cardamom into a small bowl. Add dry ingredients to creamed mixture; stir until a soft dough forms. Press into a greased 8-inch round shortbread mold or a 9-inch round cake pan. Bake 25 to 30 minutes or until lightly browned. Cool in pan 10 minutes; loosen edges with a knife. Invert onto a cutting board. If necessary, tap edge of pan on cutting board. Cut warm shortbread into wedges. Cool completely. Store in an airtight container.

Yield: 6 to 8 servings

CASHEW-FUDGE TARTS

PASTRY

- 3 cups all-purpose flour
- 6 tablespoons sugar
- 1 1/2 cups butter or margarine, softened

FILLING

- 1 can (14 ounces) sweetened condensed milk
- 1 egg
- 1 tablespoon hot water
- 1 teaspoon instant coffee granules
- 1 package (6 ounces) semisweet chocolate chips, melted
- 2 tablespoons all-purpose flour
- 1 teaspoon vanilla extract
- 1/4 teaspoon baking powder
- 1 1/2 cups lightly salted dry-roasted cashews, coarsely chopped and divided

For pastry, combine flour and sugar in a medium bowl. Using a pastry blender or 2 knives, cut butter into dry ingredients until mixture resembles coarse meal. Knead until a soft dough forms. Shape 1/2 tablespoonfuls of dough into balls. Press balls of dough into bottoms and up sides of greased miniature muffin pans.

Preheat oven to 350 degrees. For filling, whisk sweetened condensed milk and egg in a medium bowl. In a small bowl, combine water and coffee; stir until coffee dissolves. Add coffee mixture, chocolate chips, flour, vanilla, and baking powder to milk mixture; beat with an electric mixer until smooth. Stir in 1 cup cashews. Spoon about 1 tablespoon filling into each pastry. Sprinkle remaining 1/2 cup cashews evenly over filling. Bake 25 to 30 minutes or until set in center. Cool in pans 10 minutes. Transfer to a wire rack to cool completely. Store in an airtight container.

Yield: about 5 1/2 dozen tarts

CHOCOLATE TRUFFLES

- 2 2/3 cups semisweet chocolate chips, divided
- 3 tablespoons whipping cream
- 3 tablespoons crème de cassis
- 6 ounces chocolate candy coating
- 1 ounce white baking chocolate and pink paste food coloring to decorate

In top of a double boiler over warm water, melt 2 cups chocolate chips. Stir until smooth. Remove from heat and allow chocolate to cool to room temperature. Beat in whipping cream and crème de cassis until smooth. Refrigerate mixture 1 hour or until set.

Shape heaping teaspoons of mixture into 1-inch balls. Place on a baking sheet and refrigerate 30 minutes.

In top of a double boiler over hot water, melt candy coating and remaining 2/3 cup chocolate chips. Remove from heat and cool slightly. Quickly dip candies in chocolate mixture and place on waxed paper to set. Refrigerate 1 hour or until firm.

Melt white chocolate in top of double boiler over warm water. Remove chocolate from heat. Tint chocolate a pale pink. Spoon chocolate into a pastry bag fitted with a small round tip.

Pipe initials or bows onto tops of candies.

Yield: about 30 truffles

PECAN THIMBLE COOKIES

- 2 cups all-purpose flour
- 1 1/4 cups chopped pecans
- 1 cup butter, softened
- 1/4 cup granulated sugar
- 1/4 cup firmly packed brown sugar

Process flour and pecans in a food processor until pecans are very finely chopped. In a medium bowl, beat butter and sugars until light and fluffy. Stir in flour mixture. Wrap dough in plastic wrap and refrigerate overnight.

Preheat oven to 300 degrees. On a lightly floured surface, use a floured rolling pin to roll out dough to 1/4-inch thickness. Use a thimble to cut out cookies. Transfer to a foil-lined baking sheet. Bake 10 to 12 minutes or until very lightly browned.

Yield: about 50 dozen cookies

Variation: Cookies may be rolled out as directed above and cut out using desired cookie cutters. Bake 20 to 25 minutes.

Yield: about 5 dozen 2 1/2-inch cookies

Perfect for serving with coffee or tea, Pecan Thimble Cookies have a buttery brown sugar crunch. Chocolate Truffles flavored with crème de cassis are extra rich and creamy.

Dipped in candy coatings and decorated with colorful icing, Christmas Candy Canes and Christmas Dipped Cookies look — and taste — like they came from a gourmet candy shop!

CHRISTMAS DIPPED COOKIES

6 ounces chocolate candy
   coating, cut into pieces
6 ounces vanilla candy coating,
   cut into pieces
1 package (16 ounces) chocolate
   sandwich cookies
  Tubes of red, green, and white
   decorating icing

Melt chocolate and vanilla candy coating in separate small saucepans following package directions. Using tongs, dip half of cookies in chocolate candy coating. Dip remaining cookies in vanilla candy coating. Place on a wire rack to cool completely. Use decorating icing to decorate cookies. Allow icing to harden. Store in an airtight container.
Yield: 3^1/$_2$ dozen cookies

CHRISTMAS CANDY CANES

CANDY
   4   ounces chocolate candy coating
   4   ounces vanilla candy coating
  24   small peppermint candy canes

ICING
   1   cup confectioners sugar
   1   tablespoon milk
       Red and green paste food
          coloring

For candy, melt chocolate and vanilla candy coating in separate small saucepans following package directions. Using tongs, dip half of candy canes in chocolate candy coating. Dip remaining candy canes in vanilla candy coating. Place on a wire rack with waxed paper underneath to cool completely.

For icing, combine confectioners sugar and milk in a small bowl, stirring until smooth. Divide icing in half. Tint 1 bowl red and 1 bowl green. Drizzle icing over candy canes. Allow icing to harden. Store in an airtight container.

Yield: 2 dozen candy canes

NUT-CRACKER SWEETS

   1   package (12 ounces) semisweet
          chocolate chips
   3   tablespoons ground cinnamon
   1   cup unsalted cashews
   1   cup oyster crackers

Melt chocolate chips in a medium saucepan over low heat. Stir in cinnamon. Fold in cashews and crackers. Drop by heaping teaspoonfuls onto waxed paper. Cool completely. Store in an airtight container.

Yield: about 2¹/₂ dozen candies

These rich Nut-Cracker Sweets promise to be as popular as the traditional ballet character! The goodies are created by mixing cashews and oyster crackers with a combination of chocolate and cinnamon.

Light, crisp meringue filled with chocolate chips and pecans is nestled atop a chocolate crust to create Chocolate Meringue Cupcakes.

CHOCOLATE MERINGUE CUPCAKES

CRUST

16 2-inch-diameter chocolate wafer
    cookies, finely ground
 3 tablespoons butter or
    margarine, melted
 1 teaspoon ground cinnamon

FILLING

 3 egg whites
$^2/_3$ cup sugar
$^1/_2$ teaspoon ground cinnamon

$^1/_2$ cup semisweet chocolate chips
$^1/_2$ cup chopped pecans

For crust, combine cookie crumbs, butter, and cinnamon in a medium bowl; stir until well blended. Line a muffin pan with foil muffin cups. Press about 2 teaspoons mixture into bottom of each muffin cup.

Preheat oven to 325 degrees. For filling, beat egg whites in a large bowl

until foamy. Gradually adding sugar and cinnamon, beat until stiff. Fold in chocolate chips and pecans. Spoon about 2 tablespoons filling into each muffin cup. Bake 30 to 35 minutes or until lightly browned and set in center. Cool completely in pan. Store in an airtight container.

Yield: about 1$^1/_2$ dozen cupcakes

50

A batch of creamy Buttermilk Fudge makes a wonderful holiday treat. Loaded with walnuts, the old-fashioned candy has a rich caramel-like flavor that's sure to be a hit.

BUTTERMILK FUDGE

2 cups sugar
1 cup buttermilk
½ cup butter or margarine
1 tablespoon light corn syrup
1 teaspoon baking soda
1 teaspoon vanilla extract
½ cup chopped walnuts

Butter sides of a heavy large saucepan or Dutch oven. Combine sugar, buttermilk, butter, corn syrup, and baking soda in pan. Stirring constantly, cook over medium-low heat until butter melts and sugar dissolves. Using a pastry brush dipped in hot water, wash down any sugar crystals on sides of pan. Attach a candy thermometer to pan, making sure thermometer does not touch bottom of pan. Increase heat to medium and bring to a boil. Cook, without stirring, until mixture reaches soft-ball stage (approximately 234 to 240 degrees). Test about ½ teaspoon mixture in ice water. Mixture should easily form a ball in ice water but flatten when held in your hand. Remove from heat. Add vanilla; do not stir. Cool to approximately 200 degrees. Using medium speed of an electric mixer, beat until fudge thickens and begins to lose its gloss. Stir in walnuts. Pour into a buttered 8-inch square baking pan. Cool completely. Cut into 1-inch squares. Store in an airtight container in refrigerator.
Yield: about 4 dozen pieces fudge

Pretzels, toasted almonds, and dried cranberries are given a sweet, crunchy coating to create our crispy Sugared Cranberry Trail Mix.

SUGARED CRANBERRY TRAIL MIX

1 cup whole almonds
2 cups small pretzels
1 cup dried cranberries
1 egg white
1/2 cup sugar
1/2 teaspoon ground cinnamon
1/2 teaspoon salt

Preheat oven to 350 degrees. To toast almonds, spread almonds evenly on an ungreased baking sheet. Bake 7 to 8 minutes or until almonds are slightly darker in color. Cool completely on baking sheet.

Reduce oven temperature to 225 degrees. In a large bowl, combine almonds, pretzels, and cranberries. In a small bowl, beat egg white until foamy. Pour over pretzel mixture; toss until well coated. In another small bowl, combine sugar, cinnamon, and salt. Sprinkle over pretzel mixture; toss until well coated. Spread evenly on a greased baking sheet. Bake 1 hour, stirring every 15 minutes. Cool completely on baking sheet. Store in an airtight container.

Yield: about 5 cups trail mix

DRIED FRUIT-NUT ROLLS

- 1 package (8 ounces) pitted dates
- 1 package (6 ounces) dried apricots
- 1³/₄ cups flaked coconut, divided
- 1 cup chopped pecans
- 2 tablespoons firmly packed brown sugar
- 2 tablespoons orange juice
- ¹/₂ teaspoon grated orange zest

Process dates, apricots, 1 cup coconut, pecans, brown sugar, orange juice, and orange zest in a food processor until fruit and nuts are finely chopped. Shape mixture into two 6-inch-long rolls; roll in remaining ³/₄ cup coconut. Wrap in plastic wrap and store in refrigerator. Cut rolls into ¹/₄-inch slices.
Yield: 2 rolls, about 20 slices each

Deliciously rich Dried Fruit-Nut Rolls are unbelievably simple to prepare. The no-cook logs are rolled in coconut for an elegant look.

Chocolate Granola Candies are a quick-and-easy mixture of chocolate, dried fruits, and cereal. The recipe makes several dozen bite-size treats in one batch!

CHOCOLATE GRANOLA CANDIES

- 2¹/₂ cups granola cereal with fruit and nuts
- ³/₄ cup diced mixed dried fruits and raisins
- 12 ounces chocolate-flavored candy coating, cut into pieces

In a medium bowl, combine cereal and dried fruits and raisins. In a heavy medium saucepan, melt candy coating over low heat; remove from heat. Stir cereal mixture into melted chocolate. Drop teaspoonfuls of mixture into foil candy cups. Place candies in refrigerator to harden. Store in an airtight container in a cool, dry place.
Yield: about 5 dozen pieces candy

Rocky Road Candy is a nutty fudge that microwaves in minutes. Another quick-to-fix sweet is Fruitcake Cookies, a blend of fruitcake and purchased sugar cookie mix.

ROCKY ROAD CANDY

1 cup semisweet chocolate chips
1 cup milk chocolate chips
1 jar (7 ounces) marshmallow
   creme
2/3 cup sweetened condensed milk
1/2 teaspoon vanilla extract
4 cups miniature marshmallows
2 cups chopped pecans, toasted

Line a 9 x 13-inch baking pan with aluminum foil, extending foil over ends of pan; grease foil. In a 3-quart microwave-safe bowl, combine semisweet and milk chocolate chips.

Microwave on medium-high power (80%) 3 minutes, stirring after 1 1/2 minutes. Stir in marshmallow creme; microwave on medium-high power (80%) 1 minute. Add sweetened condensed milk and vanilla; stir until well blended. Add marshmallows and pecans; stir until well coated. Spread mixture into prepared pan. Chill until firm. Use ends of foil to lift candy from pan. Cut into 1-inch squares. Store in an airtight container.
Yield: about 8 dozen pieces candy

FRUITCAKE COOKIES

1 package (15 ounces) sugar
   cookie mix and ingredients
   required to prepare cookies
1 3/4 cups chopped fruitcake

Preheat oven to 375 degrees. In a medium bowl, mix cookie dough according to package directions. Stir in fruitcake pieces. Drop rounded teaspoonfuls of dough 2 inches apart onto an ungreased baking sheet. Bake 6 to 8 minutes or until edges are lightly browned. Transfer cookies to a wire rack to cool completely. Store in an airtight container.
Yield: about 4 dozen cookies

The creamy topping on our Gingerbread Bars adds a tasty twist to a traditional Christmas treat.

GINGERBREAD BARS

1 package (14.5 ounces) gingerbread cake mix
1/2 cup butter or margarine, melted
1 egg
1 package (8 ounces) cream cheese, softened
2 eggs
4 1/2 cups sifted confectioners sugar

Preheat oven to 350 degrees. In a medium bowl, combine gingerbread cake mix, butter, and 1 egg. Spread evenly into 2 greased 8-inch square baking pans. In a medium bowl, combine cream cheese, 2 eggs, and confectioners sugar. Spread evenly over gingerbread layer in each pan. Bake 30 to 35 minutes or until lightly browned. Cool completely in pans. Cut into 1 x 2-inch bars. Store in an airtight container.

Yield: about 2 dozen bars in each pan

SUGAR COOKIE ORNAMENTS

1 cup butter or margarine, softened
1½ cups sugar
1 egg
1 teaspoon vanilla extract
2¾ cups all-purpose flour
¼ teaspoon salt
1 package (10 ounces) candy-coated mini chocolate chips

Preheat oven to 350 degrees. In a large bowl, cream butter and sugar until fluffy. Add egg and vanilla; beat until smooth. In a medium bowl, combine flour and salt. Add dry ingredients to creamed mixture; stir until a soft dough forms. Shape dough into 1-inch balls and place 3 inches apart on a greased baking sheet. Press each ball into a 2½-inch-diameter circle. Use a drinking straw to make a hole in top of each cookie. Press about 1 teaspoon chocolate chips onto each cookie. Bake 8 to 10 minutes or until edges are light golden brown. Transfer to a wire rack to cool completely. Store in an airtight container.
Yield: about 5½ dozen cookies

PUMPKIN SPICE BARS

1 package (18.25 ounces) spice cake mix
1 egg
2 tablespoons butter or margarine, melted
1 package (8 ounces) cream cheese, softened
1 can (14 ounces) sweetened condensed milk
1 can (16 ounces) pumpkin
2 eggs
½ teaspoon salt
1 cup chopped pecans

Preheat oven to 350 degrees. In a large bowl, combine cake mix, 1 egg, and melted butter; stir until mixture is well blended (mixture will be dry). Press into bottom of a 10½ x 15½-inch jellyroll pan. In another large bowl, beat cream cheese until fluffy. Add sweetened condensed milk, pumpkin, 2 eggs, and salt; beat until mixture is smooth. Pour over crust. Sprinkle pecans over filling. Bake 30 to 35 minutes or until filling is set. Cool in pan on a wire rack 20 minutes; chill. Cut into 1½-inch bars. Store in an airtight container in refrigerator.
Yield: about 5 dozen bars

SNOWBALL COOKIES

3 cups finely shredded coconut
1 package (18 ounces) vanilla candy coating, cut into pieces
1 package (16 ounces) chocolate sandwich cookies

Spread coconut on waxed paper. Melt candy coating in a heavy medium saucepan over low heat. Remove from heat. Place each cookie on a fork and dip into candy coating until covered; roll in coconut. Place cookies on waxed paper and allow candy coating to harden.
Yield: about 3½ dozen cookies

GINGERBREAD REINDEER COOKIES

1 package (14 ounces) gingerbread mix
2 eggs
¼ cup vegetable oil
Small pretzel twists
Brown and red jelly beans

Preheat oven to 350 degrees. In a large bowl, combine gingerbread mix, eggs, and oil; stir until a soft dough forms. For each cookie, place a 1½-inch ball of dough on a greased baking sheet. Flatten balls into a 3-inch-high oval shape. Use fingers to press in sides of each cookie about one-third from 1 end of cookie to resemble reindeer face. Press pretzels into cookies for "antlers." Press jelly beans into cookies for "eyes" and "noses." Bake 9 to 11 minutes or until bottoms of cookies are firm. Transfer cookies to a wire rack to cool.
Yield: about 1 dozen cookies

(Clockwise from top left) *Decorated with colorful candy-coated chocolate chips, edible Sugar Cookie Ornaments can be attached to a tabletop tree using satin ribbon ties. The wintry cloaks of Snowball Cookies hide chocolaty sandwich cookies that are dipped in a melted candy coating and then rolled in coconut. These adorable Gingerbread Reindeer Cookies are made with a packaged mix and finished with pretzel antlers and candy eyes and noses. A spice-cake crust complements the flavor of creamy, easy-to-make Pumpkin Spice Bars.*

Make these sweet treats in the microwave! Creamy Lemon-Pecan Candies are made with melted marshmallows and chopped pecans, and Peanut Butter Bars have a peanut butter-graham cracker crust with a candy bar topping.

CREAMY LEMON-PECAN CANDIES

1³/₄ cups sugar
  1 cup whipping cream
  1 cup miniature marshmallows
  1 teaspoon dried lemon peel
 ¹/₂ teaspoon lemon extract
1³/₄ cups chopped pecans

In a large microwave-safe bowl, combine sugar and whipping cream. Microwave on high power (100%) 8 to 12 minutes or until mixture reaches soft-ball stage (approximately 234 to 240 degrees). Test about ¹/₂ teaspoon mixture in ice water. Mixture will easily form a ball in ice water but will flatten when held in your hand. Without scraping sides, pour candy into another large heat-resistant bowl. Add marshmallows, lemon peel, and lemon extract; beat 3 to 5 minutes or until mixture thickens and begins to lose its gloss. Stir in pecans. Quickly drop teaspoonfuls of candy onto greased waxed paper; cool completely.
Yield: about 3¹/₂ dozen pieces candy

PEANUT BUTTER BARS

  1 package (16 ounces) confectioners sugar
1¹/₂ cups graham cracker crumbs
  1 cup smooth peanut butter
  1 cup butter or margarine
  8 chocolate-covered caramel, peanut, and nougat candy bars (2.07 ounces each), chopped
  1 tablespoon milk

Combine confectioners sugar and graham cracker crumbs in a large bowl. In a medium microwave-safe bowl, combine peanut butter and butter. Microwave on medium-high power (80%) 2 minutes or until mixture melts, stirring after each minute. Pour peanut butter mixture over graham cracker mixture; stir until well blended. Press mixture into bottom of an ungreased 9 x 13-inch baking dish. Place candy bar pieces and milk in a medium microwave-safe bowl. Microwave on medium power (50%) 3 minutes or until candy melts, stirring after each minute. Spread melted candy mixture over peanut butter mixture. Cool 20 minutes or until candy mixture hardens. Cut into 1-inch squares.
Yield: about 8 dozen bars

ORANGE-DATE-NUT LOAVES

- 1 package (16 ounces) pound cake mix
- 2/3 cup vegetable oil
- 1/2 cup sweetened condensed milk
- 2 eggs
- 1 teaspoon orange extract
- 2 cups chopped pecans
- 1 package (8 ounces) chopped dates

Preheat oven to 325 degrees. In a large bowl, beat cake mix, oil, sweetened condensed milk, eggs, and orange extract at low speed of an electric mixer 30 seconds. Beat at medium speed 2 minutes. Stir in pecans and dates. Spoon batter into 2 greased and floured 5 x 9-inch loaf pans. Bake 1 hour to 1 hour 10 minutes or until a toothpick inserted in center of bread comes out with only a few crumbs attached. Cool in pans 10 minutes. Remove from pans and cool completely on a wire rack.
Yield: 2 loaves bread

BUTTERSCOTCH BRAN MUFFINS

- 1/2 cup butterscotch chips
- 4 ounces cream cheese
  Vegetable cooking spray
- 1 package (7 ounces) bran muffin mix
- 1/3 cup milk
- 1 egg, beaten

In a small saucepan, melt butterscotch chips over low heat. Stir in cream cheese until well blended; remove from heat.
Preheat oven to 400 degrees. Line 9 muffin pan cups with paper muffin cups; spray paper cups with cooking spray. In a medium bowl, combine muffin mix, milk, egg, and half of butterscotch mixture; stir just until moistened. Spoon batter into prepared muffin cups, filling each about two-thirds full. Bake 15 to 18 minutes or until a toothpick inserted in center of muffin comes out clean. Cool in pan 10 minutes; transfer muffins to a wire rack. Spread remaining butterscotch mixture over tops of warm muffins. Serve warm.
Yield: 9 muffins

Butterscotch Bran Muffins are enriched with cream cheese and butterscotch. Orange-Date-Nut Loaves add pecans, dates, and orange extract to a pound cake base.

HOLIDAY OPEN HOUSE

*B*rimming with gaiety and cheer, an open house is the perfect setting for sharing the joys of the season with friends, family, and neighbors. For an unforgettable evening, look to this fabulous collection of recipes, which features a tempting assortment of appetizers, satisfying buffet dishes, and flavorful beverages. Being the perfect holiday hostess has never been easier!

Treats for a caroling party include Honey-Walnut Crunch, Creamy White Fudge, and Cream Cheese-Topped Chocolate Cake. Hot Buttered Rum Cordial is a warming blend of cider, rum, and amaretto. (All recipes on page 62.)

HOT BUTTERED RUM CORDIAL

(Shown on page 61)

2 cups apple cider
1/2 cup firmly packed brown sugar
1/4 teaspoon ground cinnamon
1/4 teaspoon ground allspice
2 cups rum
1/4 cup amaretto
1 tablespoon butter-flavored extract

In a large saucepan, combine apple cider, brown sugar, cinnamon, and allspice. Stirring constantly, cook over medium heat until sugar dissolves. Remove from heat. Stir in rum, amaretto, and butter-flavored extract. Store in an airtight container in refrigerator 8 hours or overnight to allow flavors to blend.

Strain cordial through cheesecloth or a coffee filter. Reheat cordial; serve warm.

Yield: about 4 1/2 cups cordial

HONEY-WALNUT CRUNCH

(Shown on pages 60 and 61)

1 1/2 cups sugar
1/2 cup honey
1/2 cup corn syrup
1/4 cup water
1 cup chopped walnuts
2 tablespoons butter or margarine
1 teaspoon lemon extract
1/2 teaspoon salt
1/2 teaspoon baking soda

Butter sides of a heavy large saucepan. Combine sugar, honey, corn syrup, and water in pan. Stirring constantly, cook over medium-low heat until sugar dissolves. Using a pastry brush dipped in hot water, wash down any sugar crystals on sides of pan. Attach a candy thermometer to pan, making sure thermometer does not touch bottom of pan. Increase heat to medium and bring to a boil. Cook, without stirring, until mixture reaches hard-crack stage (approximately 300 to 310 degrees) and turns light golden in color. Test about 1/2 teaspoon mixture in ice water. Mixture should form brittle threads in ice water and remain brittle when removed from the water. Remove from heat; stir in walnuts, butter, lemon extract, and salt; stir until butter melts. Add baking soda (syrup will foam); stir until soda dissolves. Pour candy onto a large piece of buttered aluminum foil. Use 2 greased spoons to pull warm candy until stretched thin. Cool completely. Break into pieces. Store in an airtight container.

Yield: about 1 1/2 pounds candy

CREAM CHEESE-TOPPED CHOCOLATE CAKE

(Shown on page 61)

1 package (18.25 ounces) devil's food cake mix
2 eggs
1/2 cup butter or margarine, softened
2 eggs
3 1/2 cups sifted confectioners sugar
1 package (8 ounces) cream cheese, softened

Preheat oven to 350 degrees. In a large bowl, combine cake mix, 2 eggs, and butter; beat 2 minutes. Spread batter in a greased and floured 9 x 13-inch glass baking dish. In a small bowl, beat 2 eggs, confectioners sugar, and cream cheese until smooth. Spread over cake batter. Bake 35 to 40 minutes or until cake begins to pull away from sides of pan. Cool completely on a wire rack. Store in an airtight container.

Yield: about 12 servings

CREAMY WHITE FUDGE

(Shown on pages 60 and 61)

3 cups sugar
1 cup sour cream
1/3 cup light corn syrup
2 tablespoons butter or margarine
1/4 teaspoon salt
2 teaspoons vanilla extract
1 cup chopped walnuts

Butter a 7 x 11-inch baking pan. Butter sides of a large heavy saucepan or Dutch oven. Combine sugar, sour cream, corn syrup, butter, and salt in pan. Stirring constantly, cook over medium-low heat until sugar dissolves. Using a pastry brush dipped in hot water, wash down any sugar crystals on sides of pan. Attach a candy thermometer to pan, making sure thermometer does not touch bottom of pan. Increase heat to medium and bring to a boil. Cook, without stirring, until mixture reaches soft-ball stage (approximately 234 to 240 degrees). Test about 1/2 teaspoon mixture in ice water. Mixture should easily form a ball in ice water but flatten when held in your hand. Place pan in 2 inches of cold water in sink. Add vanilla; do not stir until mixture cools to approximately 200 degrees. Remove from sink. Using medium speed of an electric mixer, beat until fudge thickens and begins to lose its gloss. Stir in walnuts. Pour into prepared pan. Cool completely. Cut into 1-inch squares. Store in an airtight container in refrigerator.

Yield: about 5 dozen pieces fudge

HOT BUTTERED RUM CORDIAL

(Shown on page 61)

- 2 cups apple cider
- 1/2 cup firmly packed brown sugar
- 1/4 teaspoon ground cinnamon
- 1/4 teaspoon ground allspice
- 2 cups rum
- 1/4 cup amaretto
- 1 tablespoon butter-flavored extract

In a large saucepan, combine apple cider, brown sugar, cinnamon, and allspice. Stirring constantly, cook over medium heat until sugar dissolves. Remove from heat. Stir in rum, amaretto, and butter-flavored extract. Store in an airtight container in refrigerator 8 hours or overnight to allow flavors to blend.

Strain cordial through cheesecloth or a coffee filter. Reheat cordial; serve warm.

Yield: about 4 1/2 cups cordial

HONEY-WALNUT CRUNCH

(Shown on pages 60 and 61)

- 1 1/2 cups sugar
- 1/2 cup honey
- 1/2 cup corn syrup
- 1/4 cup water
- 1 cup chopped walnuts
- 2 tablespoons butter or margarine
- 1 teaspoon lemon extract
- 1/2 teaspoon salt
- 1/2 teaspoon baking soda

Butter sides of a heavy large saucepan. Combine sugar, honey, corn syrup, and water in pan. Stirring constantly, cook over medium-low heat until sugar dissolves. Using a pastry brush dipped in hot water, wash down any sugar crystals on sides of pan. Attach a candy thermometer to pan, making sure thermometer does not touch bottom of pan. Increase heat to medium and bring to a boil. Cook, without stirring, until mixture reaches hard-crack stage (approximately 300 to 310 degrees) and turns light golden in color. Test about 1/2 teaspoon mixture in ice water. Mixture should form brittle threads in ice water and remain brittle when removed from the water. Remove from heat; stir in walnuts, butter, lemon extract, and salt; stir until butter melts. Add baking soda (syrup will foam); stir until soda dissolves. Pour candy onto a large piece of buttered aluminum foil. Use 2 greased spoons to pull warm candy until stretched thin. Cool completely. Break into pieces. Store in an airtight container.

Yield: about 1 1/2 pounds candy

CREAM CHEESE-TOPPED CHOCOLATE CAKE

(Shown on page 61)

- 1 package (18.25 ounces) devil's food cake mix
- 2 eggs
- 1/2 cup butter or margarine, softened
- 2 eggs
- 3 1/2 cups sifted confectioners sugar
- 1 package (8 ounces) cream cheese, softened

Preheat oven to 350 degrees. In a large bowl, combine cake mix, 2 eggs, and butter; beat 2 minutes. Spread batter in a greased and floured 9 x 13-inch glass baking dish. In a small bowl, beat 2 eggs, confectioners sugar, and cream cheese until smooth. Spread over cake batter. Bake 35 to 40 minutes or until cake begins to pull away from sides of pan. Cool completely on a wire rack. Store in an airtight container.

Yield: about 12 servings

CREAMY WHITE FUDGE

(Shown on pages 60 and 61)

- 3 cups sugar
- 1 cup sour cream
- 1/3 cup light corn syrup
- 2 tablespoons butter or margarine
- 1/4 teaspoon salt
- 2 teaspoons vanilla extract
- 1 cup chopped walnuts

Butter a 7 x 11-inch baking pan. Butter sides of a large heavy saucepan or Dutch oven. Combine sugar, sour cream, corn syrup, butter, and salt in pan. Stirring constantly, cook over medium-low heat until sugar dissolves. Using a pastry brush dipped in hot water, wash down any sugar crystals on sides of pan. Attach a candy thermometer to pan, making sure thermometer does not touch bottom of pan. Increase heat to medium and bring to a boil. Cook, without stirring, until mixture reaches soft-ball stage (approximately 234 to 240 degrees). Test about 1/2 teaspoon mixture in ice water. Mixture should easily form a ball in ice water but flatten when held in your hand. Place pan in 2 inches of cold water in sink. Add vanilla; do not stir until mixture cools to approximately 200 degrees. Remove from sink. Using medium speed of an electric mixer, beat until fudge thickens and begins to lose its gloss. Stir in walnuts. Pour into prepared pan. Cool completely. Cut into 1-inch squares. Store in an airtight container in refrigerator.

Yield: about 5 dozen pieces fudge

Curry and grapes add exotic flavor to our creamy Curried Chicken Cheese Ball. It's garnished with "flowers" made from grapes and sweet red peppers.

CURRIED CHICKEN CHEESE BALLS

Curried Chicken Cheese Balls may be made one day in advance.

1 cup seedless green grapes, cut into halves
2 packages (8 ounces each) cream cheese, softened
2 cans (5 ounces each) chicken, drained
4 green onions, finely chopped

2 tablespoons sour cream
1 teaspoon curry powder
1 teaspoon seasoned salt
 Small pieces of sweet red pepper and curry powder to garnish
 Crackers or bread to serve

Reserving a few grapes to garnish, combine cream cheese, chicken,

grapes, onions, sour cream, curry powder, and seasoned salt in a large bowl; stir until well blended. Divide mixture in half and shape each half into a ball. Cover with plastic wrap and refrigerate 8 hours or overnight to allow flavors to blend.

Garnish with reserved grapes, red pepper, and curry powder. Serve with crackers or bread.

Yield: 2 cheese balls

Our mellow Havarti Fondue is especially delicious served with crispy homemade Croutons. Rich and cheesy, Spicy Crab Spread is flavored with red pepper, onions, and green pepper.

HAVARTI FONDUE WITH CROUTONS

Croutons may be made one day in advance and stored in an airtight container.

CROUTONS
- 1   loaf (about 1 pound) French bread, cut into 1-inch cubes
- 1/4 cup butter or margarine, melted
- 1/4 cup grated Parmesan cheese

FONDUE
- 1/4 cup cornstarch
- 3   tablespoons water
- 1   bottle (16 ounces) white cooking wine
- 1/2 teaspoon garlic powder
- 2   tablespoons freshly squeezed lemon juice
- 6   cups (1 1/2 pounds) shredded Havarti cheese
- 2   cups (8 ounces) shredded Gruyère cheese
- 1/3 cup cooking sherry
- 1/4 teaspoon ground white pepper

For croutons, preheat oven to 375 degrees. Place bread cubes in a large bowl. Pour melted butter evenly over bread. Sprinkle cheese over bread and toss until evenly coated. Spread evenly on an ungreased baking sheet. Stirring occasionally, bake 5 to 8 minutes or until lightly toasted. Transfer to paper towels to cool.

For fondue, dissolve cornstarch in water in a small bowl. In a large saucepan, combine wine and garlic powder. Cook over medium-low heat until heated through but not boiling. Stir in lemon juice. Gradually whisk in cheeses, whisking constantly until melted. Stir in sherry and white pepper. Gradually add cornstarch mixture and whisk until mixture begins to thicken. Pour into a fondue pot or chafing dish. Serve warm with croutons.
Yield: about 4 cups fondue

SPICY CRAB SPREAD

- 2   cans (6 ounces each) crabmeat, drained
- 1   cup (4 ounces) finely shredded sharp Cheddar cheese
- 1/2 cup mayonnaise
- 1/4 cup minced green pepper
- 2   green onions, finely chopped
- 1   teaspoon garlic powder
- 1/2 teaspoon salt
- 1/2 teaspoon dry mustard
- 1/2 teaspoon ground red pepper
      French bread or crackers to serve

In a large bowl, combine crabmeat, cheese, mayonnaise, green pepper, onions, garlic powder, salt, dry mustard, and red pepper; stir until well blended. Cover and refrigerate 2 hours. Serve chilled with French bread or crackers.
Yield: about 3 cups spread

MINIATURE CRAB CAKES WITH TARTAR SAUCE

Crab cakes may be prepared one day in advance and refrigerated until ready to bake.

TARTAR SAUCE

- 2 cups mayonnaise
- 2/3 cup finely chopped dill pickles
- 4 tablespoons freshly squeezed lemon juice
- 4 tablespoons finely minced scallions (use white and a small portion of green tops)
- 2 tablespoons drained capers, chopped
- 1/2 teaspoon creamed horseradish
- 1/2 teaspoon hot pepper sauce

CRAB CAKES

- 3 cans (6 ounces each) crabmeat, drained
- 1/2 cup finely chopped green pepper
- 1/2 cup finely chopped sweet red pepper
- 3 tablespoons minced onion
- 2 teaspoons minced fresh parsley
- 1 egg, beaten
- 1/2 cup finely crushed butter-flavored crackers (about 12 crackers)
- 1/4 teaspoon salt
- 1/8 teaspoon ground black pepper
- 3/4 cup corn flake crumbs

For tartar sauce, combine mayonnaise, pickles, lemon juice, scallions, capers, horseradish, and pepper sauce in a small bowl; stir until well blended. Reserve 1/3 cup for crab cakes; refrigerate remaining sauce until ready to serve.

Preheat oven to 350 degrees. For crab cakes, combine crabmeat, green and red peppers, onion, reserved 1/3 cup tartar sauce, parsley, egg, cracker crumbs, salt, and black pepper in a medium bowl. Carefully blend ingredients, just until mixed. Use 1 tablespoon of crab mixture to form each patty. Roll in corn flake crumbs until well coated. Place on an ungreased baking sheet. Bake 20 to 25 minutes or until golden brown. Serve warm with tartar sauce.

Miniature Crab Cakes are breaded with a crunchy corn flake coating and baked. The fresh Tartar Sauce gets its tangy flavor from dill pickles, scallions, capers, and creamed horseradish.

Yield: about 40 crab cakes and about 2 1/3 cups tartar sauce

These tasty appetizers are just right for a holiday open house. Healthy, low-fat Greek Pizza Squares feature a zippy vegetable mixture topped with two types of cheese. Marinated Shrimp Salad receives its zesty flavor from the savory herbs and spices in the marinade.

66

WINE COOLERS

1 gallon red Zinfandel wine
1 quart orange juice
1 cup freshly squeezed lemon
    juice
1/2 cup sugar
1 quart club soda, chilled
    Orange slices to serve

In a 2-gallon container, combine wine, juices, and sugar. Stir until sugar dissolves. Cover and chill.

To serve, add club soda; stir until well blended. Serve over ice with a slice of orange.

Yield: about 25 cups wine

GREEK PIZZA SQUARES

CRUST

2 cups bread flour
1 cup whole-wheat flour
1 package dry yeast
1 teaspoon sugar
1 teaspoon salt
1 1/3 cups very warm water
1 teaspoon olive oil
    Vegetable cooking spray

TOPPING

    Vegetable cooking spray
1 can (14 1/2 ounces) Italian-style
    stewed tomatoes
1/2 cup chopped onion
1/2 cup chopped green pepper
1 teaspoon fennel seed, crushed
1 teaspoon garlic powder
1 teaspoon salt
1/2 teaspoon ground black pepper
1 can (2 1/4 ounces) sliced black
    olives, drained
1 cup fat-free shredded
    mozzarella cheese
4 ounces feta cheese, crumbled

For crust, combine flours, yeast, sugar, and salt in a large bowl. Add water and oil; stir until a soft dough forms. Turn onto a lightly floured surface and knead until dough becomes smooth and elastic. Place in a large bowl sprayed with cooking spray, turning once to coat top of dough. Cover and let rise in a warm place (80 to 85 degrees) 1 hour or until doubled in size.

For topping, heat a medium skillet sprayed with cooking spray over medium heat. Add undrained tomatoes to skillet and coarsely chop. Add onion, green pepper, fennel seed, garlic powder, salt, and black pepper to skillet. Stirring occasionally, cook 5 minutes or until liquid evaporates. Remove from heat; stir in olives.

Preheat oven to 375 degrees. Turn dough onto a lightly floured surface and punch down. Press dough into a greased 10 1/2 x 15 1/2-inch jellyroll pan. Bake 10 minutes. Remove from oven. Spoon tomato mixture over crust. Sprinkle cheeses over vegetable mixture. Bake 15 to 20 minutes or until cheese is bubbly. Cut into squares and serve warm.

Yield: about 2 dozen appetizers

1 serving (2 x 3-inch piece): 88 calories, 2.0 grams fat, 4.5 grams protein, 13.5 grams carbohydrate

MARINATED SHRIMP SALAD

1/2 cup white wine vinegar
1/3 cup olive oil
6 green onions, chopped
3 tablespoons chopped fresh
    parsley
1 tablespoon garlic salt
2 teaspoons dried basil leaves,
    crushed
1/2 teaspoon ground black pepper
1 1/2 pounds large shrimp, cooked,
    peeled, and deveined
1/2 red onion, thinly sliced

In a blender or food processor, process vinegar, oil, green onions, parsley, garlic salt, basil, and pepper until well blended. In a medium bowl, combine shrimp and red onion. Pour vinegar mixture over shrimp mixture; stir until well coated. Cover and refrigerate 8 hours or overnight to allow flavors to blend. Serve chilled.

Yield: about 4 cups salad

Festively garnished with orange slices, our sparkling Wine Coolers offer fruity flavor.

These savory snacks will please guests with hearty appetites! The moist Feta Cheese Squares feature an unusual blend of cornmeal, feta cheese, and sun-dried tomatoes. Mildly spiced Sausage Bites are encased in flaky pastry.

FETA CHEESE SQUARES

1½ cups cornmeal
1½ cups water
1½ cups milk
¼ cup butter or margarine
⅓ cup finely chopped sun-dried
     tomatoes
1 cup (4 ounces) shredded sharp
     Cheddar cheese, divided
1 cup (7 ounces) finely crumbled
     feta cheese, divided
3 green onions, finely chopped
1 egg, beaten
½ teaspoon ground red pepper
½ teaspoon dried thyme leaves

Preheat oven to 400 degrees. In a small bowl, combine cornmeal and water. In a large skillet, combine milk, butter, and tomatoes. Bring to a boil; stir in cornmeal mixture. Reduce heat to medium-low. Stirring constantly, cook 5 to 7 minutes or until mixture thickens. Remove from heat. Stir in ½ cup Cheddar cheese, ½ cup feta cheese, onions, egg, red pepper, and thyme. Spoon into a greased 8 x 11-inch baking pan. Sprinkle remaining cheese evenly over top. Bake 20 to 25 minutes or until cheese begins to brown. Cut into approximately 1-inch squares and serve warm.
Yield: about 4½ dozen squares

SAUSAGE BITES

1 pound mild pork sausage
½ cup finely chopped onion
⅓ cup finely chopped green pepper
⅓ cup plain bread crumbs
1 egg
¼ cup Dijon-style mustard
1 package (17¼ ounces) frozen
     puff pastry dough, thawed
1 cup (4 ounces) shredded sharp
     Cheddar cheese
1 egg

Preheat oven to 400 degrees. In a large bowl, combine sausage, onion, green pepper, bread crumbs, and 1 egg; stir until well blended. Shape into eight 5-inch-long rolls. Place on a broiler pan and bake 30 to 35 minutes or until sausage is fully cooked and brown. Transfer to paper towels and cool to room temperature.

Preheat oven to 425 degrees. Spread mustard evenly over each pastry sheet. Sprinkle cheese evenly over mustard. Cut each pastry sheet in half from top to bottom and again from left to right. Place 1 sausage roll near 1 long edge of a pastry quarter. Roll up jellyroll style. Beat 1 egg in a small bowl. Brush edge of pastry with egg to seal. Place pastry, sealed edge down, on a greased baking sheet. Repeat for remaining sausage rolls. Bake 20 to 25 minutes or until pastry is brown. Cut into 1-inch slices and serve warm.

Yield: about 3 dozen sausage bites

CRUNCHY COLESLAW

- 6   cups shredded green cabbage
- 3/4   cup shredded carrots
- 6   green onions, chopped
- 1/2   cup sliced almonds
- 1/2   cup lightly salted roasted sunflower kernels
- 1   package (3 ounces) chicken-flavored ramen noodle soup mix
- 1/4   cup vegetable oil
- 2   tablespoons sugar
- 2   tablespoons red wine vinegar
- 1/2   teaspoon salt
- 1/2   teaspoon ground black pepper

In a large bowl, combine cabbage, carrots, onions, almonds, and sunflower kernels. In a small bowl, whisk seasoning packet from ramen noodles, oil, sugar, vinegar, salt, and pepper. Pour oil mixture over cabbage mixture; stir until well coated. Cover and chill until ready to serve.

To serve, crush ramen noodles and stir into cabbage mixture. Serve immediately.

Yield: about 7 cups coleslaw

The extra crunch in our Crunchy Coleslaw comes from almonds, sunflower kernels, and crushed ramen noodles. Red wine vinegar is the surprise ingredient in the sweet, tangy dressing.

BRIE PUFFS

1 package (17¼ ounces) frozen puff pastry dough, thawed
1 jar (12 ounces) strawberry preserves or jam
8 ounces Brie cheese, trimmed of rind and softened
2 tablespoons cooking sherry

Preheat oven to 350 degrees. On a lightly floured surface, use a 1½-inch biscuit cutter to cut out rounds from each pastry sheet. Place on an ungreased baking sheet and bake 15 to 20 minutes or until golden brown. Transfer to a wire rack to cool completely.

Carefully slice tops off puffs. Spoon about ½ teaspoon preserves onto bottom half of each puff. In a large bowl, combine cheese and sherry until well blended. Spoon about ½ teaspoon cheese mixture over preserves. Replace tops.
Yield: about 6 dozen puffs

CRANBERRY MEATBALLS

Cranberry Meatballs may be made one day in advance.

MEATBALLS

1 pound lean ground beef
¾ cup plain bread crumbs
½ cup tomato juice
2 tablespoons prepared horseradish
1 egg, beaten
1 tablespoon Worcestershire sauce
1 tablespoon minced fresh parsley
1 teaspoon salt
¼ teaspoon ground black pepper

Our Light Artichoke Spread is made with fat-free mayonnaise, so calorie-conscious guests will feel free to enjoy it. Strawberry preserves add sweetness to tiny Brie Puffs. Festive Cranberry Meatballs are served with a tangy sauce. Wassail Punch (not shown) is a warm, spicy treat for a cold evening.

SAUCE

1 tablespoon cornstarch
1 tablespoon water
1 can (16 ounces) whole berry cranberry sauce
⅓ cup firmly packed brown sugar
1 tablespoon freshly squeezed lime juice

Preheat oven to 350 degrees. For meatballs, combine meat, bread crumbs, tomato juice, horseradish, egg, Worcestershire sauce, parsley, salt, and pepper in a large bowl; stir until well blended. Shape into 1-inch balls and place in an ungreased 9 x 13-inch baking dish. Bake about 30 minutes or until meat browns. Place meatballs on paper towels to drain; set aside.

For sauce, dissolve cornstarch in water in a small bowl; stir until smooth. In a large skillet, combine cranberry sauce, brown sugar, and lime juice. Stirring constantly, cook over medium heat until sugar dissolves. Stirring constantly, add cornstarch mixture and cook until sauce thickens. Stir in meatballs. Transfer to a 2-quart casserole. Cover and refrigerate 8 hours or overnight to allow flavors to blend.

To serve, preheat oven to 350 degrees. Cover and bake 30 to 35 minutes or until heated through. Serve warm.
Yield: about 4 dozen meatballs

LIGHT ARTICHOKE SPREAD

1 can (13¾ ounces) artichoke hearts, drained and chopped
1 cup fat-free mayonnaise   .
1 cup grated Parmesan cheese
2 teaspoons garlic powder
  Crackers or bread to serve
2 fresh artichokes (optional)

Preheat oven to 350 degrees. In a medium bowl, combine artichoke hearts, mayonnaise, cheese, and garlic powder; stir until well blended. Transfer to a 1-quart casserole. Cover and bake 15 to 20 minutes or until heated through. Serve with crackers or bread.

If desired, spread may be served in fresh artichokes. To prepare artichokes, fill a large saucepan with water; bring to a boil. Add fresh artichokes and boil 5 to 8 minutes or until leaves soften. Drain and cool to room temperature. Using a sharp knife, remove stem. Leaving 2 to 3 layers of leaves, hollow out inside of each artichoke. Spoon warm spread into center of each artichoke.
Yield: about 3 cups spread

WASSAIL PUNCH

1 quart boiling water
4 spiced tea bags
1 gallon apple cider
2 quarts orange juice
1 quart cranberry juice cocktail
1½ cups sugar
12 whole cloves
1 orange
4 cinnamon sticks
½ cup small red cinnamon candies

In a stockpot, pour boiling water over tea bags; steep 4 minutes. Remove tea bags. Stir in cider, orange juice, cranberry juice, and sugar. Bring to a boil; reduce heat to a simmer. Insert cloves into orange. Add orange, cinnamon sticks, and cinnamon candies to punch. Simmer 30 minutes. Remove orange and cinnamon sticks; serve hot.
Yield: about 32 cups punch

HOT CRANBERRY-BANANA PUNCH

1 bottle (48 ounces) cranberry
   juice cocktail
1 can (6 ounces) frozen
   lemonade concentrate
1/2 cup firmly packed brown sugar
2 1/2 cups mashed bananas (about
   6 medium bananas)
1 tablespoon ground allspice
1 teaspoon ground nutmeg
1/2 teaspoon ground cinnamon

In a large saucepan or Dutch oven, combine cranberry juice, lemonade, brown sugar, and bananas. Cook over medium-high heat, stirring until well blended. Layer four 4-inch squares of cheesecloth. Place allspice, nutmeg, and cinnamon in center of cheesecloth square and tie with string; add to punch. Stirring occasionally, bring to a boil. Reduce heat to low. Cover and simmer 30 minutes. Remove spice bag. Serve hot.
Yield: about 9 cups punch

LAYERED ITALIAN LOAF

50 saltine crackers, finely ground
   (about 1 1/4 cups)
1 1/4 cups milk
1/4 cup sugar
1 teaspoon freshly squeezed
   lemon juice
1 teaspoon hot pepper sauce
1 teaspoon garlic powder
1 teaspoon salt
1/2 teaspoon ground black pepper
1/2 teaspoon dried oregano leaves
1/2 teaspoon dried basil leaves
3 eggs, beaten
1/4 cup purchased pesto sauce
1/4 cup grated Parmesan cheese
1/4 cup tomato paste

Preheat oven to 350 degrees. Line a 5 x 9-inch loaf pan with aluminum foil. Grease foil. In a large bowl, combine cracker crumbs, milk, sugar, lemon juice, pepper sauce, garlic powder, salt, pepper, oregano, and basil. Add eggs and stir until well blended. Spoon about 3/4 cup cracker mixture into each of 3 small bowls. Stir pesto sauce into first bowl of cracker mixture. Spread evenly into pan. Stir Parmesan cheese into second bowl and spread evenly over pesto layer. Stir tomato paste into third bowl and spread evenly over cheese layer. Cover with aluminum foil and bake 55 to 60 minutes or until set in center. Invert onto a serving plate; remove foil. Cut into 1/2-inch-thick slices and serve warm.
Yield: 12 to 14 servings

SWEET POTATO CRESCENT ROLLS

3 1/2 cups all-purpose flour
1/4 cup sugar
1 package dry yeast
1 teaspoon salt
1 cup butter-flavored shortening
1 can (16 ounces) sweet
   potatoes, drained and puréed
1/2 cup milk, at room temperature
1 egg
1 tablespoon vanilla extract

In a large bowl, combine flour, sugar, yeast, and salt; stir until well blended. Using a pastry blender or 2 knives, cut in shortening until mixture resembles coarse meal. Add puréed sweet potatoes, milk, egg, and vanilla; stir until a soft dough forms. Turn dough onto a lightly floured surface and knead 2 to 3 minutes or until smooth. Shape into a ball and place in a greased bowl; grease top of dough. Cover and let rise in a warm place (80 to 85 degrees) 1 hour or until doubled in size.

Preheat oven to 350 degrees. Divide dough in half and shape into 2 balls. On a lightly floured surface, use a floured rolling pin to roll out 1 ball of dough into an 8 x 10-inch rectangle. Fold in half from top to bottom and again from left to right. Roll into an 8 x 10-inch rectangle again. Referring to **Fig. 1**, cut dough into sixteen triangles. Beginning at wide end, roll up each triangle and place on an ungreased baking sheet with point side down. Repeat with remaining dough. Bake 8 to 10 minutes or until golden brown. Serve warm.
Yield: 32 rolls

Perfect for sipping on a chilly winter evening, Hot Cranberry-Banana Punch has tropical appeal. Our Layered Italian Loaf recreates Italy's tri-color flag in three spicy layers flavored with tomato, Parmesan cheese, and pesto sauce. Light and delicate, Sweet Potato Crescent Rolls offer a new twist for traditional holiday sweet potatoes.

Fig. 1

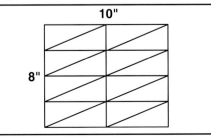

This delightful Chicken-Black Bean Casserole will bring a taste of the Southwest to a holiday potluck. Sprinkled with Parmesan cheese, Peppered Cheese Buns feature a flavorful combination of spices and robust Romano cheese.

CHICKEN-BLACK BEAN CASSEROLE

2/3 cup freshly squeezed lime juice
1/3 cup olive oil
1/2 teaspoon ground black pepper
2 teaspoons garlic powder, divided
2 teaspoons salt, divided
1 1/2 pounds boneless, skinless chicken breasts, cut into bite-size pieces
4 cups cooked white rice
2 cans (15 ounces each) black beans

1 cup finely chopped fresh cilantro
1 teaspoon onion powder
1 teaspoon chili powder
1 teaspoon ground cumin

In a medium bowl, whisk lime juice, oil, pepper, 1 teaspoon garlic powder, and 1 teaspoon salt. Add chicken; stir until evenly coated. Cover and refrigerate 2 hours.

In a 2-quart casserole, combine rice, undrained beans, cilantro, onion

powder, chili powder, cumin, remaining 1 teaspoon garlic powder, and remaining 1 teaspoon salt; set aside.

Preheat oven to 350 degrees. Using a slotted spoon, place chicken in a large skillet. Cook over medium heat until juices run clear when chicken is pierced with a fork. Stir chicken into rice mixture. Cover and bake 40 to 45 minutes or until heated through.
Yield: about nine 1-cup servings

74

PEPPERED CHEESE BUNS

- 1 package dry yeast
- 1 cup warm water
- 3 cups all-purpose flour
- ½ cup grated Romano cheese
- 2 tablespoons sugar
- 1 teaspoon garlic powder
- 1 teaspoon onion powder
- 1 teaspoon ground black pepper
- ½ teaspoon salt
- 1 tablespoon olive oil
  Vegetable cooking spray
  Grated Parmesan cheese

In a small bowl, combine yeast and warm water; stir until yeast dissolves. In a medium bowl, combine flour, Romano cheese, sugar, garlic powder, onion powder, pepper, and salt. Add yeast mixture and oil to dry ingredients. Stir until a soft dough forms. Turn onto a lightly floured surface and knead about 5 minutes or until dough becomes smooth and elastic. Place in a medium bowl sprayed with cooking spray, turning once to coat top of dough. Cover and let rise in a warm place (80 to 85 degrees) 1 hour or until doubled in size.

Turn dough onto a lightly floured surface and punch down. For each bun, shape about 3 tablespoons dough into a 4-inch-long roll. Tie each roll into a knot and place on a greased baking sheet. Spray tops of buns with cooking spray, cover, and let rise in a warm place 30 minutes or until doubled in size.

Preheat oven to 375 degrees. Bake 12 to 15 minutes or until golden brown. Transfer to a wire rack. Lightly spray buns with cooking spray; sprinkle with Parmesan cheese. Allow to cool completely. Store in an airtight container.

Yield: about 3½ dozen buns

A holiday party isn't complete without rich, creamy Southern Eggnog.

SOUTHERN EGGNOG

You'll love our eggnog. It begins with a cooked custard made in advance. We've also included a version for those who prefer eggnog without alcohol.

- 1 cup sugar, divided
- 12 large eggs, separated
- ½ teaspoon salt
- 1 quart milk
- ¼ cup water
- ¾ teaspoon cream of tartar
- 2 cups whipping cream
- ½ cup brandy
- ½ cup dark rum
  Freshly grated nutmeg

In top of a double boiler, combine ½ cup sugar, egg yolks, and salt. Gradually stir in milk. Cook over simmering water until mixture thickens and coats the back of a metal spoon. Remove from heat and cool. Pour mixture into an airtight container and chill.

In top of double boiler, combine egg whites, remaining ½ cup sugar, water, and cream of tartar. Whisking constantly, cook over simmering water until a thermometer reaches 160 degrees (about 10 minutes). Transfer egg white mixture to a large bowl; beat until stiff peaks form. Cover and chill mixture.

In a large bowl, beat whipping cream until stiff peaks form. Pour egg yolk mixture into punch bowl. Stir in brandy and rum. (For eggnog without alcohol, omit brandy and rum; stir in 2 teaspoons rum extract and 1 cup whipping cream.) Fold in egg white mixture and whipped cream. Sprinkle with nutmeg.

Yield: about 3½ quarts eggnog

Miniature Bacon-Cheese New Potatoes are savory twice-baked treats. A sassy alternative to ordinary dips, Tomatillo Salsa is an unusual Mexican snack. Thin and crispy, Spicy Corn Wafers are perfect for nibbling or dipping.

SPICY CORN WAFERS

1 1/2 cups white cornmeal
1 teaspoon garlic powder
3/4 teaspoon salt
1/2 teaspoon ground red pepper
2 1/4 cups boiling water
4 tablespoons butter or margarine, melted

Preheat oven to 425 degrees. In a medium bowl, combine cornmeal, garlic powder, salt, and red pepper. Stirring constantly, pour boiling water over dry ingredients and mix well; stir in melted butter. For each wafer, drop 1 tablespoon batter onto an ungreased nonstick baking sheet. Using back of spoon, spread batter to form a 3-inch circle; add hot water to thin batter if necessary. Bake 18 to 20 minutes or until edges are golden brown. Serve warm.

Yield: about 3 dozen wafers

BACON-CHEESE NEW POTATOES

1½ pounds small unpeeled new
    potatoes
2 tablespoons olive oil
1 cup (2 ounces) finely shredded
    Gruyère cheese
½ cup sour cream
½ cup minced green onions
    (about 3 large onions)
1 package (3 ounces) cream
    cheese, softened
2 tablespoons minced fresh basil
    or 1 teaspoon dried basil
    leaves
1 clove garlic, minced
¼ teaspoon salt
¼ teaspoon ground black pepper
8 ounces bacon, cooked and
    finely chopped

Preheat oven to 400 degrees. Rub potatoes with oil and place on an ungreased baking sheet; bake 1 hour or until tender. Allow potatoes to cool enough to handle. Cut potatoes in half. Cut a small slice from bottom of each potato half. Using a small melon baller, scoop out a small portion of potato pulp, leaving at least a ¼-inch shell; reserve potato pulp.

In a medium bowl, beat potato pulp, Gruyère cheese, sour cream, green onions, cream cheese, basil, garlic, salt, and pepper with an electric mixer; stir in bacon. Spoon potato mixture into each potato shell; place on a greased baking sheet. Broil 5 to 7 minutes or until lightly browned. Serve warm.
Yield: about 26 potato halves

TOMATILLO SALSA

1 small onion, quartered
¼ cup water
¼ teaspoon salt
1¼ pounds fresh tomatillos,
    husked and washed (about
    12 tomatillos)
½ cup coarsely chopped green
    pepper

A frothy combination of cherry and coconut flavors, Merry Cherry Cocktails are laced with rum and brandy. Dollops of whipped cream and maraschino cherries make festive garnishes.

2 jalapeño peppers, seeded
2 tablespoons chopped fresh
    cilantro
1 tablespoon freshly squeezed
    lime juice
1 clove garlic, coarsely chopped
    Tortilla chips to serve

In a medium saucepan, combine onion, water, and salt over medium heat; cover and cook about 5 minutes or until onion is soft. Add whole tomatillos, green pepper, and jalapeño peppers to saucepan. Reduce heat, cover, and cook 15 minutes or until tomatillos are tender; drain. Process tomatillo mixture, cilantro, lime juice, and garlic in a food processor until coarsely chopped. Pour into a serving dish; cover and allow to stand 1 hour for flavors to blend. Serve at room temperature with tortilla chips.
Yield: about 3 cups salsa

MERRY CHERRY COCKTAILS

⅔ cup half and half
½ cup cream of coconut
⅓ cup dark rum
⅓ cup cherry brandy
3 tablespoons maraschino
    cherry juice
3 teaspoons grenadine syrup
1½ to 2 cups ice cubes
    Whipped cream and
    maraschino cherries to
    garnish

Place half and half, cream of coconut, rum, brandy, cherry juice, grenadine, and ice in a blender; process until well blended. Pour into glasses; garnish each serving with whipped cream and a cherry.
Yield: 5 to 6 servings

MINI CHEDDAR SOUFFLÉS

- 1 pound white potatoes, peeled and cut into pieces
- 1/4 cup butter or margarine
- 1/4 cup all-purpose flour
- 6 eggs, separated
- 1/2 teaspoon salt
- 1/4 teaspoon ground black pepper
- 1/4 teaspoon cream of tartar
- 1 3/4 cups (7 ounces) shredded sharp Cheddar cheese

In a large saucepan, cover potatoes with salted water. Bring water to a boil and cook 25 to 30 minutes or until potatoes are tender. Drain, reserving 1 1/2 cups potato water. Process potatoes in a food processor until puréed; leave in processor.

Preheat oven to 375 degrees. In a large saucepan, melt butter over medium heat. Add flour, stirring until smooth. Cook 3 to 4 minutes or until flour begins to brown. Whisk in reserved potato water. Bring to a boil. Stirring occasionally, reduce heat to low and simmer 5 minutes. Add sauce to potato purée and process until well blended. Transfer to a large bowl; whisk in egg yolks, salt, and pepper. In another large bowl, beat egg whites and cream of tartar until stiff peaks form. Fold half of egg white mixture into potato mixture. Fold in cheese and remaining egg white mixture. Spoon into a heavily greased miniature muffin pan, filling each cup three-fourths full. Bake 25 to 30 minutes or until golden brown. Serve warm.

Yield: about 7 dozen mini soufflés

SPICY BLACK BEAN DIP

Spicy Black Bean Dip may be made one day in advance.

- 3 cans (15 ounces each) black beans, drained
- 1/2 cup peeled and coarsely chopped cucumber
- 1/4 cup finely chopped fresh cilantro
- 2 tablespoons minced sweet red pepper
- 2 tablespoons minced sweet yellow pepper
- 2 tablespoons minced green pepper
- 2 tablespoons minced red onion
- 2 tablespoons freshly squeezed lime juice
- 1 jalapeño pepper, seeded
- 2 teaspoons dried basil leaves
- 1 teaspoon ground black pepper
- 1/2 teaspoon garlic powder
- 1/2 teaspoon ground cumin
- 1/4 teaspoon salt
- 1/4 teaspoon hot pepper sauce
- 1/4 cup shredded sharp Cheddar cheese to garnish
  Tortilla chips or crackers to serve

Process beans, cucumber, cilantro, red pepper, yellow pepper, green pepper, onion, lime juice, jalapeño pepper, basil, black pepper, garlic powder, cumin, salt, and pepper sauce in a food processor until puréed. Transfer to a 1 1/2-quart casserole dish. Cover and refrigerate 8 hours or overnight to allow flavors to blend.

To serve, preheat oven to 350 degrees. Cover and bake 15 to 20 minutes or until heated through. Sprinkle cheese over bean dip. Serve with chips or crackers.

Yield: about 4 1/2 cups bean dip

RASPBERRY CORDIAL

- 1 package (12 ounces) frozen red raspberries, thawed
- 3 cups apple juice
- 1 cup rum
- 2/3 cup crème de cassis
- 1/2 cup raspberry-flavored liqueur
- 1/3 cup sugar

Process raspberries in a food processor until puréed. Strain; discard seeds. In a 2-quart container, combine puréed raspberries, apple juice, rum, crème de cassis, raspberry-flavored liqueur, and sugar; stir until well blended. Cover and refrigerate. Serve chilled.

Yield: about 6 cups cordial

Mini Cheddar Soufflés are light, fluffy little tidbits. Rum gives extra holiday spirit to sweet Raspberry Cordial. Enhanced with fresh vegetables, Spicy Black Bean Dip brings south-of-the-border style to your celebration.

SPICY ROASTED PEANUTS

- 2 tablespoons vegetable oil
- 4 cloves garlic, minced
- 1 tablespoon crushed red pepper flakes
- 2 cans (16 ounces each) salted peanuts
- 2 teaspoons paprika
- 1 teaspoon chili powder

Preheat oven to 350 degrees. In a heavy large skillet, cook oil, garlic, and red pepper flakes over medium heat about 1 minute. Remove from heat. Add peanuts and stir until well coated. Pour peanut mixture onto a baking sheet. Stirring occasionally, bake about 20 minutes or until lightly browned. Sprinkle paprika and chili powder over peanuts and stir. Allow peanuts to cool completely.
Yield: about 6 cups peanuts

HUMMUS DIP

- 2 cans (15 ounces each) chick-peas, drained
- 1/2 cup olive oil
- 3 tablespoons freshly squeezed lemon juice
- 2 cloves garlic, coarsely chopped
- 1 tablespoon tahini (ground sesame seed)
- 1 tablespoon coarsely chopped onion
- 1 tablespoon minced fresh parsley
- 1/4 teaspoon salt
- 1/4 teaspoon ground black pepper
- 1/8 teaspoon curry powder
  Sliced black olives, fresh parsley, and red onion wedges to garnish
  Pita bread triangles to serve

Process chick-peas, oil, lemon juice, garlic, tahini, onion, parsley, salt, pepper, and curry powder in a food processor until smooth. Spoon hummus into a serving dish. Garnish with black olives, parsley, and red onion wedges. Serve at room temperature with pita bread triangles.
Yield: about 3 cups dip

Spicy Roasted Peanuts are coated with garlic, red pepper flakes, chili powder, and paprika. Hummus Dip is a creamy Middle Eastern substitute for bean dip that's delicious served with pita triangles.

80

Stuffed Grapes with Lemon Cream and Cranberry-Topped Brie are colorful appetizers — and rich in taste!

CRANBERRY-TOPPED BRIE

Cranberries add a tangy-sweet flavor that will make this baked cheese recipe a favorite for entertaining all year long.

- 1/3 cup purchased cranberry-orange sauce
- 2 tablespoons firmly packed brown sugar
- 1 tablespoon brandy
- 1/4 cup chopped pecans
- 1 round (2 pounds) Brie cheese Artificial holly to decorate Crackers to serve

Preheat oven to 500 degrees. In a small bowl, combine cranberry-orange sauce, brown sugar, and brandy. Stir in pecans; set aside.

Cutting to within 1/4-inch of outside edge, remove rind from top of cheese. Place cheese on a glass pie plate. Spread cranberry mixture over top of cheese. Bake 5 to 8 minutes or until cheese is heated through, but not melted. Decorate with artificial holly. Serve warm with crackers.
Yield: 12 to 15 servings

STUFFED GRAPES WITH LEMON CREAM

This refreshing hors d'oeuvre offers a light change from the heartier party foods.

- 1 package (8 ounces) cream cheese, softened
- 1/3 cup sifted confectioners sugar
- 1 tablespoon freshly squeezed lemon juice
- 1 teaspoon grated lemon zest
- 1 pound large red or green seedless grapes

In a medium bowl, beat cream cheese, confectioners sugar, lemon juice, and lemon zest until smooth. Cover and chill 2 hours.

Use a sharp knife to cut an "X" through top of each grape, being careful not to cut through bottom. Spread sections apart slightly. Spoon cream cheese mixture into a pastry bag fitted with a medium star tip. Pipe mixture into each grape. Grapes may be prepared and refrigerated up to 4 hours before serving.
Yield: about 3 1/2 dozen grapes

VEGETABLE PATÉ

2 packages (8 ounces each) Neufchâtel cheese, softened
3/4 cup fat-free sour cream
2 tablespoons all-purpose flour
4 eggs
2 cloves garlic, minced
2 tablespoons freshly squeezed lemon juice
1 teaspoon chili powder
1 teaspoon salt
1/2 teaspoon ground black pepper
1/4 teaspoon paprika
1/4 teaspoon hot pepper sauce
1 cup (4 ounces) shredded sharp Cheddar cheese
1/2 cup finely chopped broccoli
1/2 cup peeled and finely chopped carrots
1/4 cup finely chopped green onions
1 cup chopped tomato
2 teaspoons dried parsley flakes
Crackers or bread to serve

Preheat oven to 375 degrees. In a large bowl, beat Neufchâtel cheese, sour cream, and flour using an electric mixer. Add eggs, 1 at a time, beating well after each addition. Add garlic, lemon juice, chili powder, salt, pepper, paprika, and pepper sauce; stir until well blended. Fold in Cheddar cheese, broccoli, carrots, and green onions. Pour into a greased 9-inch springform pan. Bake 35 to 45 minutes or until set in center. Cool completely on a wire rack. Remove sides of pan, cover, and refrigerate until well chilled.

To serve, place tomato on top of paté. Lightly sprinkle with parsley flakes. Serve with crackers or bread.
Yield: about 16 servings

This creamy Vegetable Paté gets its garden-fresh goodness from bits of broccoli, carrot, onion, and tomato. Green olives lend distinctive flavor to Olive-Cream Cheese Bagels.

OLIVE-CREAM CHEESE BAGELS

1 cup milk, scalded
1 package (3 ounces) cream cheese, softened
1/4 cup butter or margarine
1 tablespoon sugar
1 teaspoon salt
1 package dry yeast
2 eggs
1/2 cup sliced green olives
4 cups all-purpose flour
Cream cheese to serve

In a medium saucepan, combine milk, cream cheese, butter, sugar, and salt. Cook over medium-low heat, stirring occasionally, until mixture reaches 115 degrees. Remove from heat; transfer to a large bowl. Add yeast and stir until dissolved. Let stand 3 minutes. Whisk eggs into milk mixture. Stir in olives. Gradually stir in flour. Turn onto a lightly floured surface and knead 5 to 10 minutes or until dough becomes smooth and elastic. Shape into a ball and place in a greased bowl. Grease top of dough, cover, and let rise in a warm place (80 to 85 degrees) 30 minutes.

Turn dough onto a lightly floured surface and punch down. For each bagel, pinch off about 2 tablespoons dough and shape into a 5-inch-long roll. Form dough into a ring, overlap ends, and pinch ends to seal. (Or, using a floured rolling pin, roll out dough to 1/2-inch thickness. Use a 2-inch biscuit cutter to cut out dough. Use the end of a wooden spoon to punch a hole through center of each bagel.) Place on a greased baking sheet. Cover and let rise in a warm place 10 minutes or until puffy.

Preheat oven to 400 degrees. Fill a large saucepan with water; bring to a boil. Drop 4 to 5 bagels at a time into boiling water and cook 3 minutes, turning once. Transfer to a greased baking sheet. Bake 25 to 30 minutes or until golden brown. Serve warm or at room temperature with cream cheese.
Yield: about 2 1/2 dozen bagels

BLACKBERRY CORDIAL

2/3 cup crème de cassis
1/2 cup raspberry-flavored liqueur
1/2 cup blackberry-flavored brandy
1 cup club soda, chilled
Frozen blackberries to garnish

In a 1-quart container, combine crème de cassis, liqueur, and brandy; stir until well blended. Cover and chill until ready to serve.

To serve, add club soda and pour cordial over ice. Garnish with frozen blackberries.
Yield: about 6 servings

Sparkling Blackberry Cordial has a fruity kick.

CREAMY CHICKEN-MUSHROOM DIP

1 can (10³/₄ ounces) golden mushroom soup, undiluted
1 package (8 ounces) cream cheese, softened
1 can (5 ounces) chunk white chicken, drained
¹/₂ cup sliced fresh mushrooms
¹/₂ cup slivered almonds, toasted
2 tablespoons white wine
1 small clove garlic, minced
¹/₈ teaspoon ground white pepper
Chips or crackers to serve

In a heavy medium saucepan, combine soup and cream cheese. Stir over medium heat until smooth. Add chicken, mushrooms, almonds, wine, garlic, and white pepper; stir until well blended and heated through. Serve warm with chips or crackers.
Yield: about 2¹/₂ cups dip

MUSTARD ROLLS

2 packages dry yeast
¹/₄ cup warm water
1 tablespoon sugar
1 cup milk
²/₃ cup prepared mustard
2 tablespoons butter or margarine
4 cups all-purpose flour
Vegetable cooking spray
1 egg yolk
1 tablespoon water

In a small bowl, combine yeast, ¹/₄ cup warm water, and sugar; stir until well blended. In a small saucepan, heat milk, mustard, and butter over medium-high heat until butter melts. In a large bowl, combine yeast mixture, milk mixture, and flour. Stir until a soft dough forms. Turn onto a lightly floured surface and knead about 8 minutes or until dough becomes smooth and elastic. Place in a large bowl sprayed with cooking spray, turning once to coat top of dough. Cover and let rise in a warm place (80 to 85 degrees) 1 hour or until doubled in size.

Turn dough onto a lightly floured surface and punch down. Shape dough into 1¹/₂-inch balls and place 2 inches apart on a greased baking sheet. Lightly spray tops of rolls with cooking spray. Cover and let rise in a warm place 1 hour or until doubled in size.

Preheat oven to 400 degrees. In a small bowl, whisk egg yolk with 1 tablespoon water; brush over tops of rolls. Bake 12 to 15 minutes or until golden brown. Serve warm with Herbed Beef Brisket.
Yield: about 3¹/₂ dozen rolls

HERBED BEEF BRISKET

4 pound beef brisket
12 to 15 cloves garlic, thinly sliced
3 tablespoons fennel seed
1 tablespoon all-purpose flour
1 cup hot water
1 teaspoon beef bouillon granules
2 tablespoons Worcestershire sauce
1 teaspoon dried marjoram leaves
1 teaspoon dried thyme leaves
1 teaspoon ground oregano
1 teaspoon ground black pepper
Mustard Rolls (recipe on this page) and desired condiments to serve

Preheat oven to 325 degrees. Trim excess fat from brisket. Make ¹/₂-inch-deep cuts in meat across the grain. Insert garlic slices into cuts. Sprinkle fennel seed over top of brisket. Place flour in a large (14 x 20-inch) oven cooking bag; shake to coat bag. Place brisket in bag. Pour water into a small bowl; dissolve bouillon in water. Add Worcestershire sauce, marjoram, thyme, oregano, and pepper to bouillon mixture; pour into cooking bag. Seal and puncture cooking bag according to package directions. Bake 2¹/₄ to 2¹/₂ hours or until tender. Allow meat to stand in bag 10 to 15 minutes. Remove meat from bag; thinly slice across the grain. Serve warm on Mustard Rolls with desired condiments.
Yield: 30 to 40 appetizers

Toasted almonds are a pleasant surprise in Creamy Chicken-Mushroom Dip. Robust Mustard Rolls are the perfect accompaniment for Herbed Beef Brisket. Sure to satisfy hearty appetites, the tender meat is stuffed with sliced garlic and sprinkled with fennel seeds that impart an aromatic flavor.

PASTA ROLLS WITH MARINARA SAUCE

Pasta Rolls and Marinara Sauce may be made one day in advance.

MARINARA SAUCE

 2 tablespoons olive oil
 ½ cup finely chopped onion
 1 clove garlic, minced
 1 can (29 ounces) tomato sauce
 1 can (14½ ounces) Italian-style stewed tomatoes
 ½ cup grated Parmesan cheese
 1 teaspoon dried parsley flakes
 1 teaspoon sugar
 ½ teaspoon dried oregano leaves
 ½ teaspoon dried basil leaves
 ½ teaspoon dried thyme leaves
 ½ teaspoon salt
 ¼ teaspoon ground black pepper

PASTA ROLLS

 2 tablespoons olive oil
 ½ cup butter or margarine, divided
 1 cup finely chopped onion
 2 cloves garlic, minced
 2 packages (10 ounces each) frozen chopped spinach, thawed and drained
 1 cup ricotta cheese
 1 cup grated Parmesan cheese
 1 teaspoon salt
 ½ teaspoon ground black pepper
 ½ teaspoon ground nutmeg
 1 package (16 ounces) lasagna noodles

Pasta Rolls filled with spinach and cheeses make impressive hors d'oeuvres. They're served with homemade Marinara Sauce, a zesty blend of tomatoes, onion, garlic, and Italian spices.

For marinara sauce, combine oil, onion, and garlic in a large saucepan. Sauté over medium heat until onion is tender. Add tomato sauce, tomatoes, cheese, parsley flakes, sugar, oregano, basil, thyme, salt, and pepper; stir until well blended. Bring to a boil. Reduce heat to low, cover, and simmer 25 to 30 minutes. Pour sauce into a 9 x 13-inch baking dish; set aside.

For pasta rolls, heat oil and ¼ cup butter in a large skillet over medium heat until butter melts. Add onion and garlic; sauté until onion is tender. Add spinach and continue to cook 10 to 15 minutes or until all liquid has evaporated. Remove from heat and cool to room temperature.

In a large bowl, combine ricotta cheese, Parmesan cheese, salt, pepper, and nutmeg; stir until well blended. Stir in spinach mixture; set aside.

Fill a large saucepan or Dutch oven with water; bring to a boil. Add noodles and cook 8 to 10 minutes or until tender. Drain and rinse with cold water. Spread about 2 tablespoons spinach mixture evenly on each noodle. Use a sharp knife to cut each noodle in half from top to bottom and again from left to right. Beginning with 1 short edge, roll up each piece jellyroll style. Standing rolls on 1 end, place in sauce. Cover and refrigerate 8 hours or overnight to allow flavors to blend.

To serve, preheat oven to 350 degrees. Cover with aluminum foil and bake 25 to 30 minutes or until heated through. Melt remaining ¼ cup butter in a small saucepan over medium heat. Brush butter lightly over pasta rolls. Serve warm.
Yield: about 6 dozen pasta rolls

MICROWAVE CARAMEL CORN

Vegetable cooking spray
16 cups popped popcorn, popped without fat or salt
1 cup firmly packed brown sugar
2 tablespoons light corn syrup
2 tablespoons molasses
1/2 teaspoon salt
1/2 teaspoon baking soda
1/2 teaspoon vanilla extract

Spray inside of a 14 x 20-inch oven cooking bag with cooking spray. Place popcorn in bag. In a 2-quart microwave-safe bowl, combine brown sugar, corn syrup, and molasses. Microwave on high power (100%) 2 minutes or until mixture boils. Stir and microwave on high power 2 minutes longer. Stir in salt, baking soda, and vanilla. Pour syrup over popcorn; stir and shake until well coated. Microwave on high power 1 1/2 minutes. Stir, shake, and microwave 1 1/2 minutes longer. Spread on aluminum foil sprayed with cooking spray. Cool completely. Store in an airtight container.
Yield: about 16 cups caramel corn

1 serving (1 cup caramel corn): 90 calories, 0 gram fat, 1.0 gram protein, 21.8 grams carbohydrate

FUDGE MELTAWAYS

3/4 cup butter or margarine, divided
3 ounces unsweetened baking chocolate, chopped and divided
1 1/2 cups finely crushed vanilla wafers
1 cup flaked coconut
1/2 cup chopped pecans
1/4 cup granulated sugar
1 egg
2 teaspoons vanilla extract, divided
2 cups sifted confectioners sugar
3 tablespoons milk

For a tree-trimming party, take along these quick-to-fix treats. Chewy Sesame Candy has a deliciously different taste. Coconut and pecans lend extra appeal to delectable Fudge Meltaways. Microwave Caramel Corn is a great fat-free snack.

Preheat oven to 350 degrees. Stirring constantly, melt 1/2 cup butter and 1 ounce chocolate in a large saucepan over low heat. Remove from heat; stir in cookie crumbs, coconut, pecans, granulated sugar, egg, and 1 teaspoon vanilla. Press into a buttered 7 x 11-inch baking pan. Bake 8 minutes. Cool completely.
Stirring constantly, melt remaining 1/4 cup butter and 2 ounces chocolate in a medium saucepan over low heat. Remove from heat; stir in confectioners sugar, milk, and remaining 1 teaspoon vanilla. Spread over crumb mixture in pan. Cool completely. Cut into 1-inch squares.
Yield: about 5 dozen candies

SESAME CANDY

1 cup sesame seed, divided
1 cup old-fashioned oats
1 cup sifted confectioners sugar
3/4 cup nonfat dry milk powder
3/4 cup smooth peanut butter
1/2 cup honey
2 tablespoons water
1 teaspoon vanilla extract

Preheat oven to 350 degrees. Spread sesame seed on an ungreased baking sheet. Stirring occasionally, bake 5 to 8 minutes or until lightly browned. Cool completely on pan.
In a medium bowl, combine 1/4 cup sesame seed, oats, confectioners sugar, dry milk, peanut butter, honey, water, and vanilla; stir until well blended. Shape into 1-inch balls. Roll in remaining 3/4 cup sesame seed. Cover and refrigerate.
Yield: about 6 dozen pieces candy

FESTIVE FAMILY FEASTS

*W*elcome the family home for the holidays with generous portions from our sumptuous dinner collection. You can choose from four complete menus, including two with international appeal, or you can mix and match favorite recipes to create your own exciting array of flavors. Whether it's served on Christmas Day, Christmas Eve, or some other time during the season, this year's family feast will be the most memorable one ever!

Basted and baked to a golden brown, Ginger-Glazed Turkey (recipe on page 90) looks picture-perfect. A bed of Apple Rings with Sweet Potato Topping (recipe on page 91) is an attractive and pleasantly sweet way to combine two traditional flavors.

For your convenience, we've provided two complete menus for a special holiday dinner —
or you can create your own tasty combination from the many delicious offerings.

MENU 1

Sweet Red Pepper-Crab Bisque

Cherry Salad

Ginger-Glazed Turkey

Apple Rings with Sweet Potato Topping

Cranberry-Filled Stuffing Ring

Cranberry-Apple Relish

Honey-Glazed New Potatoes

Asparagus en Croûte with Tarragon Sauce

Cheddar-Pumpkin Soufflé

Lemon Mousse with Raspberry Sauce

MENU 2

Cardinal Cocktails

Lobster Salad with Creamy Dressing

Roast Duckling with Berry Sauce

Holiday Rice

Glazed Baked Onions

Baked Pineapple Oranges

Broccoli Timbales

Zucchini-Carrot au Gratin

Easy Pumpernickel Bread

Cranberry Crème Brûlée

GINGER-GLAZED TURKEY (Shown on pages 88 and 89)

GLAZE
- 6 tablespoons finely chopped crystallized ginger
- 1/4 cup vegetable oil
- 1 cup soy sauce
- 6 tablespoons firmly packed brown sugar
- 6 tablespoons rum

TURKEY
- 13 to 15 pound turkey
- 2 tablespoons vegetable oil
- Salt and ground black pepper
- 1 cup water

GRAVY
- 1 tablespoon cornstarch
- 2 tablespoons water

For glaze, combine ginger and oil in a medium saucepan. Cook over medium heat until ginger begins to brown. Stir in soy sauce, brown sugar, and rum. Bring to a boil; remove from heat.

For turkey, remove giblets and neck from turkey. Place giblets and neck in a medium saucepan and add enough water to cover; bring to a boil. Continue to boil 20 minutes; remove from heat. Cover saucepan, cool 10 minutes, and refrigerate.

Preheat oven to 350 degrees. Rinse turkey and pat dry with paper towels. Rub turkey with oil. Liberally salt and pepper turkey inside and out. Tie ends of legs to tail with kitchen twine; lift wing tips up and over back so they are tucked under bird. Place in a large roasting pan with breast side up. Insert a meat thermometer into thickest part of thigh without touching bone. Pour 1 cup water into pan. Brush glaze on turkey. Loosely cover with aluminum foil and roast 3 to 3 1/2 hours, basting with glaze every 30 minutes.

To test for doneness, meat thermometer should register 180 degrees and juices run clear when thickest part of thigh is pierced with a fork. Transfer turkey to a serving platter and let stand 20 minutes before carving. Reserve remaining glaze and 1 cup drippings from roasting pan for gravy.

For gravy, dissolve cornstarch in water in a small bowl. Pour remaining glaze and reserved drippings into saucepan containing giblet mixture. Bring to a boil over medium heat. Remove neck and giblets. Stirring constantly, add cornstarch mixture and continue to cook 5 to 8 minutes or until gravy thickens. Serve with turkey.
Yield: 18 to 20 servings

APPLE RINGS WITH SWEET POTATO TOPPING

(Shown on pages 88 and 89)

SWEET POTATO TOPPING

- 1 can (29 ounces) sweet potatoes, drained
- 1 tablespoon butter or margarine, melted
- 1 tablespoon firmly packed brown sugar
- 1/4 teaspoon salt
- 1/8 teaspoon ground cloves
- 1/8 teaspoon ground cinnamon

APPLE RINGS

- 6 tablespoons butter or margarine
- 1/4 cup firmly packed brown sugar
- 2 tablespoons water
- 2 tablespoons freshly squeezed lemon juice
- 1 teaspoon dried lemon peel
- 1/2 teaspoon ground ginger
- 3 unpeeled Red Delicious apples (about 1 1/4 pounds), cored and cut into 1/2-inch rings (about 20 rings)

For sweet potato topping, process sweet potatoes, melted butter, brown sugar, salt, cloves, and cinnamon in a food processor until smooth. Transfer to a medium saucepan. Stirring occasionally, cook over medium heat 10 to 12 minutes or until heated through. Remove from heat, cover, and set aside.

For apple rings, melt butter in a large skillet over medium heat. Add brown sugar, water, lemon juice, lemon peel, and ginger; stir until sugar dissolves. Cook 1 layer of apple rings at a time 5 to 6 minutes in sugar mixture; turn and cook 5 to 6 minutes longer or until tender. Arrange on serving platter. If necessary, reheat sweet potato topping over low heat, stirring occasionally. Spoon sweet potato topping into a pastry bag fitted with a large star tip and pipe in center of each apple ring. Serve warm.

Yield: about 10 servings

This chilled Cherry Salad features fruity taste and creamy texture.

CHERRY SALAD

- 2 cups boiling water
- 2 packages (3 ounces each) cherry gelatin
- 1 can (16 ounces) pitted cherries packed in water, drained
- 1 pint vanilla ice cream, softened
- 1 cup sour cream
  Whipped cream to garnish

In a large bowl, combine boiling water and gelatin; stir until gelatin dissolves. Cool to room temperature.

Purée cherries in a food processor. Add to gelatin mixture; stir until well blended. In a medium bowl, beat ice cream and sour cream using medium speed of an electric mixer. Stir ice cream mixture into gelatin mixture. Pour into a 9 x 13-inch baking pan. Cover and refrigerate until set. Cut into 3-inch squares and garnish with whipped cream.

Yield: about 12 servings

Cranberries and horseradish bring a distinctive taste to corn bread dressing in this Cranberry-Filled Stuffing Ring. Small chunks of tomato and pepper add color to Sweet Red Pepper-Crab Bisque.

SWEET RED PEPPER-CRAB BISQUE

Bisque may be made one day in advance.

2 tablespoons olive oil
3 cups coarsely chopped sweet red peppers (about 3 large sweet red peppers)
3 green onions, chopped
1 cup coarsely chopped celery (about 3 ribs celery)
2/3 cup coarsely chopped carrots (about 2 medium carrots)
1/2 cup coarsely chopped red onion
2 teaspoons salt

1/2 teaspoon dried tarragon leaves
1/8 teaspoon ground red pepper
4 cups coarsely chopped tomatoes (about 4 large tomatoes)
1 1/2 cups whipping cream
1 cup dry sherry
2 tablespoons rum
1/2 pound lump crabmeat
1/2 teaspoon freshly squeezed lemon juice or to taste

In a 6-quart saucepan, heat oil over medium heat. Add sweet red peppers, green onions, celery, carrots,

red onion, salt, tarragon, and ground red pepper; cook, stirring occasionally, until vegetables are tender. Add tomatoes; stir until well blended. Stir in whipping cream, sherry, and rum. Reduce heat to low and simmer 1 hour, stirring occasionally. Stir in crabmeat and lemon juice; cook 5 to 10 minutes longer or until crabmeat is heated through. Serve warm. (If making bisque in advance, cover and refrigerate. Reheat over low heat until warm.)
Yield: 8 to 10 servings

CRANBERRY-FILLED STUFFING RING

CRANBERRY FILLING
1 can (16 ounces) whole berry
    cranberry sauce
1/4 cup prepared horseradish
2 tablespoons sour cream

STUFFING
3/4 cup butter or margarine
3 cups coarsely chopped onions
    (about 2 large onions)
1 cup coarsely chopped celery
    (about 3 ribs celery)
4 cups corn bread crumbs
5 slices white bread, torn into
    small pieces (about 4 cups)
2 tablespoons rubbed sage
2 teaspoons poultry seasoning
1 teaspoon salt
1/2 teaspoon ground black pepper
4 eggs, beaten
1 can (14 1/2 ounces) chicken
    broth

For cranberry filling, combine cranberry sauce, horseradish, and sour cream in a medium saucepan. Bring to a boil over medium heat. Continue to cook, stirring occasionally, 10 to 12 minutes or until filling begins to thicken. Remove from heat; set aside.

For stuffing, melt butter in a large skillet over medium heat. Add onions and celery; sauté until tender. Remove from heat. In a large bowl, combine corn bread crumbs, white bread, sage, poultry seasoning, salt, and pepper. Stir in onion mixture, eggs, and chicken broth.

Preheat oven to 350 degrees. Spread half of stuffing into a heavily greased 10-inch springform tube pan. Bake 30 minutes. Pour filling evenly over baked stuffing. Spread remaining stuffing evenly over filling. Bake 45 to 55 minutes longer or until top is brown. Loosen sides of pan. Invert onto a serving plate. Slice and serve immediately.
Yield: 12 to 16 servings

Chopped apples and sliced carrots lend a crunchy, sweet flavor to Holiday Rice.

HOLIDAY RICE

1 1/4 cups uncooked long-grain rice
2 tablespoons butter
2 cups chicken broth
1/2 cup water
1 1/2 teaspoons sugar
3/4 teaspoon rubbed sage
1/2 teaspoon salt
1/2 teaspoon ground black pepper
1 unpeeled small red apple, cored
    and chopped
1 unpeeled small green apple,
    cored and chopped
2 ribs celery, thinly sliced
3/4 cup thinly sliced carrots
1/3 cup half and half
1/3 cup sliced almonds
1/4 cup golden raisins

In a heavy large skillet, lightly brown rice in butter. Add chicken broth, water, sugar, sage, salt, and pepper. Bring to a boil; cover, reduce heat, and simmer 15 minutes. Stir in apples, celery, carrots, half and half, almonds, and raisins; cook 3 minutes longer. Serve warm.
Yield: 6 to 8 servings

Roast Duckling with Berry Sauce makes a savory, elegant entrée. For a rich aperitif or after-dinner drink, serve Cardinal Cocktails, a blend of red wine and raspberry liqueur.

ROAST DUCKLING WITH BERRY SAUCE

Berry Sauce may be made one day in advance and refrigerated.

- 1 package (16 ounces) frozen blackberries, thawed
- 4 to 5 pound duckling
- 3 tablespoons butter or margarine
- 4 tablespoons olive oil, divided
- 6 green onions, chopped
- 4 cloves garlic, minced
- 2 cans (14 1/2 ounces each) chicken broth
- 1 1/2 cups chopped carrots (about 2 large carrots)
- 2/3 cup chopped celery (about 2 ribs celery)
- 1/4 cup corn syrup
- 1/4 cup soy sauce
- 1 tablespoon red wine vinegar
- 1 tablespoon cornstarch
- 2 tablespoons water

Reserve 8 to 10 blackberries to garnish. Purée remaining blackberries in a food processor. Strain purée and set aside; discard seeds.

Remove and reserve wings, neck, and giblets from duckling. In a large saucepan, combine butter and 2 tablespoons oil over medium heat. Add green onions and garlic; sauté until onions are tender. Add wings, neck, and giblets; sauté until brown. Stir in chicken broth, carrots, and celery; bring to a boil. Reduce heat to low and simmer about 20 minutes. Add corn syrup, soy sauce, vinegar, and blackberry purée to broth mixture. Bring to a boil over medium heat, stirring constantly. Reduce heat to low and simmer 20 minutes. Remove wings, neck, and giblets. Purée sauce in batches in food processor; set aside.

Preheat oven to 375 degrees. Rinse duckling and pat dry with paper towels. Rub duckling with remaining 2 tablespoons oil and place on a meat rack in a large roasting pan. Bake uncovered 1 hour. Basting every 30 minutes with sauce, cover and bake 1 to 1 1/2 hours longer or until juices run clear when thickest part of thigh is pierced with a fork. Transfer duckling to serving platter.

To thicken sauce, dissolve cornstarch in water in a small bowl to make a thin paste. Transfer remaining sauce to a medium saucepan; bring to a boil. Add cornstarch mixture to sauce and cook 5 to 7 minutes, stirring constantly, until thickened and heated through. Serve warm over duckling. Garnish with reserved blackberries.
Yield: about 6 servings

CRANBERRY-APPLE RELISH

- 2 cups sugar
- 2 cups water
- 4 cups fresh or frozen cranberries
- 1 unpeeled apple, cored and finely chopped
- 1/2 cup raisins
- 1 teaspoon grated orange zest

In a large saucepan, bring sugar and water to a boil over medium-high heat. Boil 5 minutes. Add cranberries and chopped apple; boil 10 to 15 minutes longer or until cranberries pop and mixture begins to thicken. Remove from heat; stir in raisins and orange zest. Cover and cool.
Yield: about 4 1/2 cups relish

CARDINAL COCKTAILS

- 1 cup crème de cassis
- 2 cups Beaujolais wine

Combine crème de cassis and wine in a 1-quart pitcher; stir until well blended. Cover and refrigerate. Serve chilled.
Yield: 3 cups cocktail

Cranberry-Apple Relish is a tangy alternative to traditional cranberry sauce.

LOBSTER SALAD WITH CREAMY DRESSING

Creamy Dressing may be made one day in advance.

CREAMY DRESSING

- 3/4 cup olive oil
- 1/4 cup white wine vinegar
- 1/4 cup sour cream
- 1/4 cup whipping cream
- 3 tablespoons Dijon-style mustard
- 2 green onions, chopped
- 1 teaspoon garlic powder
- 1 teaspoon dried lemon peel
- 1 teaspoon salt
- 1/2 teaspoon ground black pepper

LOBSTER SALAD

- 3 lobster tails (about 8 ounces each)
- 1 pound bacon, cooked and crumbled
- 1 head romaine lettuce, torn into small pieces
- 1 small red onion, chopped
- 2 large tomatoes, cut into wedges
  Green onions to garnish

For dressing, process oil, vinegar, sour cream, whipping cream, mustard, green onions, garlic powder, lemon peel, salt, and pepper in a food processor until smooth. Cover and refrigerate 8 hours or overnight to allow flavors to blend.

For salad, plunge lobster tails into enough boiling, salted water to cover. Bring to a rolling boil again. Boil 10 to 15 minutes or until lobster turns pink; drain. Plunge lobster into cold water and drain again. Cover and refrigerate until well chilled. Remove lobster meat from shells and cut meat into 1/2-inch slices. Cover and refrigerate until ready to serve.

In a large bowl, toss bacon, lettuce, red onion, and tomato. Divide salad evenly into 8 bowls. Arrange 3 to 4 pieces of lobster on top of each salad. Spoon about 2 tablespoons dressing over each salad. Garnish with green onion.
Yield: 8 servings

Our Lobster Salad with Creamy Dressing offers a refreshing way to start a meal. The delicate dressing is a delightful complement to the lobster.

BAKED PINEAPPLE ORANGES

This tart orange cup may be prepared ahead. We garnished the scalloped edges of the oranges with finely minced parsley.

- 6 large navel oranges
- 4 cups crushed pineapple with juice
  Juice of 1 lemon
- 1/2 cup granulated sugar
- 1/4 cup firmly packed light brown sugar
- 1/4 cup sherry
- 1/2 teaspoon ground nutmeg
- 1/2 cup finely chopped walnuts

Cut oranges in half and scoop out pulp; reserve orange shells and pulp. Scallop edges of orange shells.

Preheat oven to 350 degrees. In a large saucepan, combine orange pulp, undrained pineapple, lemon juice, and sugars. Stirring frequently, cook over low heat until thickened.

Elegant individual portions make these Glazed Baked Onions and Baked Pineapple Oranges irresistible.

Stir in sherry and nutmeg. Spoon orange mixture into shells and sprinkle with chopped walnuts. Bake 20 minutes. Serve at room temperature.
Yield: 12 servings

GLAZED BAKED ONIONS

This is a good make-ahead recipe.

  4   medium onions
       Chicken broth
  2   packages (10 ounces each)
       frozen green peas, cooked

  $1/2$ cup soft bread crumbs
  5   tablespoons butter or margarine
  $1/4$ cup grated Parmesan cheese
  2   tablespoons chopped fresh
       parsley
  $1/2$ teaspoon dry mustard
       Melted butter or margarine
       Pimiento strips to garnish

  Peel and halve onions. Place in a large saucepan in 2 inches of chicken broth. Bring to a boil, cover, and reduce heat. Simmer 20 minutes or until onions are tender but still firm; drain well. Gently lift out centers of

onions, leaving a shell 2 to 3 layers thick. Fill centers with peas. Combine bread crumbs, 5 tablespoons butter, Parmesan cheese, parsley, and dry mustard. Sprinkle mixture over onions. Drizzle with melted butter. (To serve later, cover onions and chill.) Broil 5 to 7 minutes or until lightly browned. Garnish with pimiento strips.
Yield: 8 servings

Make holiday dinners special with fancy side dishes. Honey-Glazed New Potatoes get a hint of sweetness from honey. Gruyère cheese gives Zucchini-Carrot au Gratin its distinctive savor. Fluffy Broccoli Timbales are well seasoned with garlic.

98

ZUCCHINI-CARROT AU GRATIN

3 cups thinly sliced carrots (about 4 large carrots)
7 cups sliced zucchini (about 2 pounds)
1/4 cup butter or margarine, cut into small pieces
1 teaspoon salt
1/2 teaspoon ground black pepper
6 ounces Gruyère cheese, shredded
1/2 cup chicken broth

In a large saucepan, cover carrots with water. Bring water to a boil and cook carrots 3 to 5 minutes or until just tender; drain.

Preheat oven to 375 degrees. Place zucchini in a greased 9 x 13-inch glass baking dish. Place carrots over zucchini. Place pieces of butter evenly over carrots. Sprinkle salt, pepper, and cheese evenly over vegetables. Pour chicken broth evenly over top. Cover and bake 20 minutes. Bake uncovered 25 to 30 minutes longer or until cheese browns and vegetables are tender. Serve warm.
Yield: 8 to 10 servings

BROCCOLI TIMBALES

1 package (16 ounces) frozen chopped broccoli, thawed
1 clove garlic
1 1/4 cups whipping cream
2 eggs
1/2 teaspoon dried basil leaves
1/2 teaspoon dried thyme leaves
1/2 teaspoon salt
1/4 teaspoon ground black pepper

Preheat oven to 325 degrees. Process broccoli and garlic in a food processor until finely chopped. Add whipping cream, eggs, basil, thyme, salt, and pepper; process until puréed. Spoon mixture evenly into 6 custard cups or small ramekins.

Place cups in a 9 x 13-inch baking pan and fill pan with hot water to come halfway up sides of cups. Bake 50 to 55 minutes or until a toothpick inserted in center of cups comes out clean. Serve warm.
Yield: 6 servings

HONEY-GLAZED NEW POTATOES

2 1/2 pounds new potatoes, cut into quarters
1/2 cup butter or margarine
1/4 cup water
2 tablespoons honey
1 teaspoon salt
1/4 teaspoon ground black pepper

In a large saucepan or Dutch oven, cover potatoes with salted water. Bring water to a boil and cook until potatoes are tender; drain.

In a large skillet, melt butter over medium heat. Stir in water, honey, salt, and pepper. Stirring occasionally, cook 1 layer of potatoes at a time 10 to 12 minutes or until brown. Transfer to serving dish and cover with aluminum foil to keep warm. Serve warm.
Yield: 6 to 8 servings

EASY PUMPERNICKEL BREAD

1 package (16 ounces) hot roll mix
3/4 cup warm (105 to 115 degrees) strongly brewed coffee
2 eggs
1/4 cup molasses
3/4 cup rye flour
3 teaspoons caraway seed, divided
2 teaspoons cocoa
Vegetable cooking spray
1 egg white, lightly beaten

In a small bowl, sprinkle yeast from roll mix over coffee; allow yeast to soften. Stir in eggs and molasses. In a medium bowl, combine roll mix, rye flour, 2 teaspoons caraway seed, and cocoa. Add yeast mixture; stir until a soft dough forms. Place in a large bowl sprayed with cooking spray, turning once to coat top of dough. Cover and let rise in a warm place (80 to 85 degrees) about 1 hour or until doubled in size.

Turn dough onto a lightly floured surface and knead 3 minutes or until dough becomes smooth and elastic. Shape dough into 2 round loaves and place on a greased baking sheet. Spray tops of dough with cooking spray, cover, and let rise in a warm place 1 hour or until doubled in size.

Preheat oven to 350 degrees. Brush dough with egg white and sprinkle with remaining 1 teaspoon caraway seed. Bake 25 to 30 minutes or until bread is golden brown and sounds hollow when tapped. Transfer to a wire rack to cool completely. Store in an airtight container.
Yield: 2 loaves bread

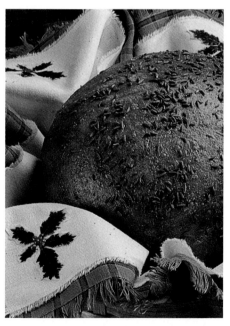

Sprinkled with caraway seed, Easy Pumpernickel Bread is a hearty addition to a meal.

ASPARAGUS EN CROÛTE WITH TARRAGON SAUCE

Tarragon Sauce may be made one day in advance.

ASPARAGUS EN CROÛTE

- 1 cup water
- 3 packages (8 ounces each) frozen asparagus spears, cut into 4-inch spears
- 1 can (8 ounces) refrigerated crescent rolls
- 2 tablespoons butter or margarine, melted

TARRAGON SAUCE

- 1/2 cup butter or margarine
- 2 tablespoons all-purpose flour
- 1 tablespoon Dijon-style mustard
- 1/2 teaspoon dried tarragon leaves, crushed
- 1/2 teaspoon salt
- 1/4 teaspoon ground black pepper
- 1 cup whipping cream

For asparagus en croûte, bring water to a rolling boil in a large skillet. Add asparagus; cook 5 to 8 minutes or until tender. Drain well and pat dry with paper towels.

Preheat oven to 375 degrees. Separate crescent rolls into triangles. Stack about 5 spears of asparagus on wide end of each triangle. Beginning with wide end, roll up each triangle and place on an ungreased baking sheet with point side down. Brush asparagus and crescent roll with melted butter. Bake 10 to 13 minutes or until rolls are golden brown.

For tarragon sauce, melt butter in a medium saucepan over medium heat while asparagus-crescent rolls are baking. Add flour, mustard, tarragon, salt, and pepper to melted butter; stir to form a thin paste. Slowly stir in whipping cream. Cook, stirring constantly, 5 to 8 minutes or until sauce thickens. (If making sauce in advance, cover and refrigerate. To reheat, transfer to a saucepan and cook over medium-low heat until warm.)

To serve, spoon about 2 tablespoons sauce onto each plate. Place asparagus-crescent roll on top of sauce. Serve immediately.

Yield: 8 servings

CHEDDAR-PUMPKIN SOUFFLÉ

- 1/3 cup grated Parmesan cheese
- 1/4 cup butter or margarine
- 1/4 cup all-purpose flour
- 1 1/2 cups water
- 1 can (16 ounces) pumpkin
- 6 eggs, separated
- 1/2 teaspoon salt
- 1/4 teaspoon ground black pepper
- 1/4 teaspoon cream of tartar
- 1 3/4 cups (about 7 ounces) shredded sharp Cheddar cheese

Prepare a 1 1/2-quart soufflé dish by fitting an aluminum foil collar around outside of dish with top extending 3 to 4 inches above rim. Use transparent tape to secure. Grease dish and collar. Dust dish and collar with Parmesan cheese; discard excess.

Preheat oven to 400 degrees. In a large saucepan, melt butter over medium heat. Add flour, stirring to make a paste. Cook 3 to 4 minutes or until flour begins to brown. Whisk in water. Stirring constantly, bring to a boil and cook 5 minutes. Add pumpkin and stir until well blended. Remove from heat.

Place egg yolks in a large bowl. Whisk about 1/2 cup pumpkin mixture into yolks. Whisk salt, pepper, and remaining pumpkin mixture into yolk mixture.

In another large bowl, beat egg whites and cream of tartar until stiff. Fold 1/2 of egg white mixture into pumpkin mixture. Fold Cheddar cheese and remaining egg white mixture into pumpkin mixture. Pour into soufflé dish. Bake 1 hour 10 minutes to 1 hour 15 minutes or until brown and set in center. Remove collar and serve immediately.

Yield: 10 to 12 servings

Cheddar-Pumpkin Soufflé is light and savory. Wrapped in flaky crescent rolls and served atop a delicious sauce, asparagus becomes especially appealing in Asparagus en Croûte with Tarragon Sauce.

Complete a memorable meal with one of these creamy and colorful desserts. The zesty flavor of cranberries balances the richness of custard in our Cranberry Crème Brûlée. Individual portions of tangy Lemon Mousse with Raspberry Sauce are shaped in muffin cups.

102

CRANBERRY CRÈME BRÛLÉE

Cranberry Crème Brûlée may be made one day in advance.

1 cup dried cranberries (available at gourmet food stores)
1 cup orange-flavored liqueur
5 egg yolks
1/3 cup granulated sugar
1 1/2 cups whipping cream
1/4 cup milk
1/4 teaspoon ground cinnamon
1/4 cup firmly packed brown sugar

Combine cranberries and liqueur in a small bowl; cover and set aside overnight.

Preheat oven to 325 degrees. Beat egg yolks and granulated sugar in a large bowl until well blended using an electric mixer. Beat in whipping cream, milk, and cinnamon. Pour mixture evenly into 6 custard cups. Place cups in a 9 x 13-inch baking pan and fill pan with hot water to come halfway up sides of cups. Bake 1 hour to 1 hour 5 minutes or until custard is set in center. Transfer cups to a wire rack to cool completely. Cover and refrigerate until chilled.

Preheat broiler. Place cups in a 9 x 13-inch baking pan and fill pan with hot water to come halfway up sides of cups. Drain cranberry mixture and spoon berries evenly over each custard. Sprinkle about 2 teaspoons brown sugar over each custard. Broil about 1 minute or until sugar caramelizes. Serve immediately.
Yield: 6 servings

LEMON MOUSSE WITH RASPBERRY SAUCE

Lemon Mousse and Raspberry Sauce may be made one day in advance and stored in separate containers in the refrigerator.

LEMON MOUSSE
1 1/2 teaspoons unflavored gelatin
2 tablespoons cold water
3/4 cup freshly squeezed lemon juice
3/4 cup sugar
4 eggs
3 tablespoons butter or margarine
2 tablespoons grated lemon zest
1 cup whipping cream

RASPBERRY SAUCE
2 packages (12 ounces each) frozen red raspberries, thawed
1 bottle (1 1/2 liters) Beaujolais wine
1 cup sugar

For lemon mousse, place a large bowl and beaters from an electric mixer in refrigerator until well chilled. In a small bowl, sprinkle gelatin over water; allow to stand 1 minute to soften. In top of a double boiler over simmering water, whisk lemon juice, sugar, eggs, butter, and lemon zest. Stir in gelatin mixture. Stirring constantly, cook over simmering water 8 to 10 minutes or until lemon mixture thickens and coats the back of a spoon. Remove from heat and cool to room temperature.

In chilled bowl, beat whipping cream until stiff. Gently fold into lemon mixture. Spoon evenly into 12 paper-lined muffin cups. Cover and refrigerate until set.

For raspberry sauce, purée raspberries in a food processor. Strain purée; discard seeds. Combine purée, wine, and sugar in a heavy large saucepan. Cook over medium-high heat, stirring until sugar dissolves and mixture begins to boil. Reduce heat to medium-low and simmer about 3 hours or until mixture reduces to about 2 cups. Remove from heat, cover, and refrigerate until well chilled.

To serve, invert onto a serving plate and remove paper from each mousse. Spoon about 2 1/2 tablespoons sauce over each mousse. Serve chilled.
Yield: 12 servings

INTERNATIONAL SAMPLER DINNERS

These menus are great for dinner parties! You can serve one of two complete menus
or mix and match your favorites to create an unforgettable holiday meal.

<table>
<tr><td>

MENU 1

Curry-Mushroom Soup

Frosty Cranberry Tiptops

Rack of Lamb with Olive Stuffing

Eggplant Napoleon

Green Bean Sauté

Spinach-Squash Casserole

Tzimmes

Challah

Mousse au Chocolate

</td><td>

MENU 2

Tortilla Soup

Pork Loin Roast in White Wine

Chinese Rice Ring with Broccoli

English Christmas Cabbage

Winter Vegetable Trio

Benne Seed Cookies

Chocolate Rum Balls

Chocolate-Raspberry Cake

</td></tr>
</table>

An impressive addition to your holiday table, tender Rack of Lamb is seasoned with garlic and rosemary. Flavorful Olive Stuffing is the perfect accompaniment to this Greek entrée.

RACK OF LAMB WITH OLIVE STUFFING

LAMB

- 8 cloves garlic, divided
- 2 tablespoons finely chopped fresh parsley
- 1 tablespoon dried rosemary leaves
- 1 tablespoon olive oil
  Salt and ground black pepper
- 2 racks of lamb (approximately 2 pounds per rack), frenched with fat trimmed to 1/4-inch thickness
- 3 tablespoons Dijon-style mustard
- 1/4 cup butter or margarine
- 1/2 cup plain bread crumbs
- 3 cups water

STUFFING

- 1/4 cup butter or margarine
- 3 cups coarsely chopped onions
- 1 cup coarsely chopped celery
- 2 tablespoons ground sage
- 2 tablespoons dried rosemary leaves
- 1 tablespoon dried thyme leaves
- 2 teaspoons poultry seasoning
- 1 teaspoon salt
- 1/2 teaspoon ground black pepper
- 4 cups corn bread crumbs
- 5 slices white bread, torn into small pieces (about 4 cups)
- 1 cup finely chopped green olives
- 1 jar (3 1/2 ounces) capers, drained
- 1 can (14 1/2 ounces) chicken broth
- 4 eggs, beaten
  Fresh rosemary to garnish

For lamb, finely chop 7 cloves of garlic. In a small bowl, combine chopped garlic, parsley, rosemary, and oil. Rub garlic mixture over all sides of lamb. Cover and refrigerate overnight.

Preheat oven to 350 degrees. For stuffing, melt butter in a large skillet over medium heat. Add onions and celery; cook until tender. Remove from heat. Process sage, rosemary, thyme, poultry seasoning, salt, and pepper in a small food processor until mixture is a fine powder. In a large bowl, combine corn bread crumbs, white bread, olives, capers, and herb mixture. Stir in onion mixture, chicken broth, and eggs. Spoon into a greased 9 x 13-inch pan, cover, and bake 50 minutes. Uncover and bake 10 minutes longer or until top is golden brown. Remove from oven, cover, and keep warm.

Increase oven temperature to 450 degrees. Sprinkle salt and pepper over all sides of lamb. Heat a large heavy skillet over medium-high heat. Place lamb in skillet, fat side down, and cook until fat is browned. Remove from heat. Place racks of lamb, fat side up, in a shallow roasting pan. Insert a meat thermometer into lamb without touching bone or fat. Spread mustard over fat side of lamb. Mince remaining garlic. In same skillet, melt butter over medium heat. Stir garlic into butter and cook until garlic begins to brown. Remove from heat; stir in bread crumbs. Press bread crumb mixture into mustard on lamb. Pour water into roasting pan. Cover lamb and roast about 1 hour or until thermometer reaches 175 degrees. Arrange racks of lamb on a serving plate. Fill inside of racks with stuffing. Garnish with fresh rosemary. Slice individual rib sections and serve with additional stuffing.

Yield: 6 to 8 servings

SPINACH-SQUASH CASSEROLE

- 6 medium yellow squash, sliced
- 2 packages (10 ounces each) frozen chopped spinach, thawed and drained
- 1 package (8 ounces) cream cheese, softened
- 2 eggs, lightly beaten
- 6 tablespoons butter or margarine, melted
- 1 tablespoon sugar
- 1/2 teaspoon salt
- 1/2 teaspoon garlic salt
- 1 teaspoon ground black pepper
- 1 cup cheese cracker crumbs
- 6 slices bacon, cooked and crumbled
  Paprika

Preheat oven to 350 degrees. Cook squash in salted boiling water until tender (about 10 minutes); drain. Place squash in a large bowl and mash. Add spinach, cream cheese, eggs, melted butter, sugar, salt, garlic salt, and pepper to squash; stir until well blended. Pour into a lightly greased 2-quart baking dish; top with cracker crumbs, bacon, and paprika. Cover and bake 45 minutes. Remove cover and bake 15 minutes longer or until center is set. Serve warm.

Yield: 8 to 10 servings

Bacon and cheese cracker crumbs top our Spinach-Squash Casserole.

Curry-Mushroom Soup makes a zesty first course with its Indian flavor. Garnished with crispy crumbled bacon, the delicious soup features mushrooms, spinach, and onions.

CURRY-MUSHROOM SOUP

3/4 cup butter or margarine, divided
4 cups (about 12 ounces) sliced fresh mushrooms
1 cup finely chopped onion
1/3 cup all-purpose flour
3 tablespoons curry powder
2 teaspoons garlic powder
2 teaspoons salt
1/2 teaspoon ground black pepper
4 cups milk
2 cups whipping cream
1 package (10 ounces) frozen chopped spinach, thawed and drained
6 slices bacon, cooked and crumbled

In a large skillet, melt 1/4 cup butter over medium heat. Add mushrooms and onion; cook until tender. Remove from heat. In a Dutch oven, melt remaining 1/2 cup butter over medium heat. Stir in flour, curry powder, garlic powder, salt, and pepper. Cook 2 minutes. Whisking constantly, gradually add milk and whipping cream and cook until thickened. Stir in mushroom mixture and spinach. Cook until heated through. Sprinkle bacon over each serving of soup.
Yield: about nine 1-cup servings

PORK LOIN ROAST IN WHITE WINE

2 cups dry white wine
1/4 cup frozen orange juice concentrate, thawed
1/2 cup finely chopped fresh parsley
2 teaspoons rubbed sage
1 teaspoon dried rosemary leaves
3 to 3 1/2 pound pork loin roast on the bone
Salt and ground black pepper
3 cloves garlic, thinly sliced
3 cups water
Orange slices and fresh parsley to garnish

Prepared in the French style, this handsome Pork Loin Roast in White Wine is wonderfully moist and tender. The succulent roast is marinated in a mixture of white wine, herbs, and orange juice before baking.

Whisk wine, orange juice, parsley, sage, and rosemary in a medium bowl. Sprinkle all sides of roast with salt and pepper. Use a sharp knife to make slits in roast; place garlic slices into slits. Place roast in a 1-gallon resealable plastic bag. Reserving 1 cup marinade, pour remaining marinade over roast. Seal bag and refrigerate 8 hours or overnight, turning several times.

Preheat oven to 350 degrees. Place roast, fat side up, in a shallow baking pan. Pour water into pan. Insert a meat thermometer into roast without touching bone or fat. Roast about 1 1/2 hours, basting every 30 minutes with reserved marinade. If necessary, add more wine to marinade.

Reduce oven temperature to 325 degrees. Continue roasting 30 to 40 minutes longer or until meat thermometer registers 170 degrees and juices run clear when roast is pierced with a fork. Transfer roast to a serving platter and garnish with orange slices and parsley. Let stand 10 minutes before carving.
Yield: about 6 servings

Whipped potatoes, turnips, and rutabagas make Swedish Winter Vegetable Trio a hearty side dish. Topped with chunky tomato sauce and fresh oregano, Eggplant Napoleon has a spicy Italian flavor.

EGGPLANT NAPOLEON

SAUCE

- ½ cup finely chopped onion
- 1 clove garlic, minced
- 2 tablespoons olive oil
- 1 can (29 ounces) tomato sauce
- 1 can (14½ ounces) Italian-style stewed tomatoes, chopped
- ½ cup grated Parmesan cheese
- 1 teaspoon dried parsley flakes
- 1 teaspoon sugar
- ½ teaspoon dried oregano leaves
- ½ teaspoon dried basil leaves
- ½ teaspoon dried thyme leaves
- ½ teaspoon salt
- ¼ teaspoon ground black pepper

EGGPLANT

- 3 eggplants, divided
- ½ pound fresh mushrooms
- 1 teaspoon salt
- 1 teaspoon ground black pepper
- 2 tablespoons olive oil
- 1 cup plain bread crumbs
- ½ cup grated Parmesan cheese
- ½ teaspoon garlic powder
- ½ cup all-purpose flour
- 4 eggs, beaten
  Vegetable oil
  Fresh oregano to garnish

For sauce, cook onion and garlic in oil in a large saucepan over medium heat until onion is tender. Add tomato sauce, tomatoes, Parmesan cheese, parsley, sugar, oregano, basil, thyme, salt, and pepper; stir until well blended. Bring to a boil, reduce heat to low, cover, and simmer 30 minutes.

For eggplant, peel and coarsely chop 1 eggplant. While sauce is simmering, purée chopped eggplant, mushrooms, salt, and pepper in a food processor. In a medium skillet, heat olive oil over medium heat. Add eggplant mixture; cook until all liquid has evaporated. Remove eggplant mixture and sauce from heat, cover, and set aside.

Peel and slice remaining 2 eggplants into ¼-inch-thick slices (about 24 slices). In a medium bowl, combine bread crumbs, cheese, and garlic powder. Place flour and eggs in separate small bowls. Dip each slice of eggplant into flour and then egg; coat well with bread crumb mixture. In a large skillet, fry eggplant slices in hot vegetable oil in batches until golden brown on both sides. Transfer to paper towels to drain.

If necessary, rewarm sauce and puréed mixture. To serve, spread puréed mixture between 3 slices of fried eggplant and place on serving plate. Spoon about ¼ cup sauce over eggplant. Repeat with remaining ingredients. Garnish with fresh oregano. Serve immediately.
Yield: about 8 servings

WINTER VEGETABLE TRIO

- 2 pounds rutabagas, peeled and quartered
- 2 pounds turnips, peeled and quartered
- 2 pounds russet potatoes, peeled and quartered
- 1 cup butter or margarine, softened
- 1 cup whipping cream
- 2 teaspoons salt
- 1 teaspoon ground black pepper
  Shredded Cheddar cheese and chopped fresh parsley to garnish

In an 8-quart stockpot, cover rutabagas with salted water. Bring to a boil and cook 15 minutes. Add turnips, potatoes, and enough water to cover vegetables. Bring to a boil again and cook until vegetables are tender; drain.

Transfer vegetables to a very large bowl. Add butter, whipping cream, salt, and pepper. Using an electric mixer, beat vegetables until light and fluffy. Garnish with cheese and parsley.
Yield: about 16 servings

FROSTY CRANBERRY TIPTOPS

This beautiful layered salad can be made in advance and frozen in convenient paper cups.

- 1 can (16 ounces) jellied cranberry sauce
- 1 can (8 ounces) crushed pineapple, drained
- 3 tablespoons freshly squeezed lemon juice
- 1 cup whipping cream
- ½ cup sifted confectioners sugar
- 1 package (3 ounces) cream cheese, softened
- ⅓ cup mayonnaise
- 1 cup chopped pecans or walnuts
  Whipped cream and fresh cranberries to garnish

In a medium bowl, break up cranberry sauce with a fork. Add pineapple and lemon juice; mix thoroughly. In a large bowl, beat whipping cream until stiff peaks form. Beat confectioners sugar, cream cheese, and mayonnaise into whipped cream. Fold in pecans. Spoon a layer of cranberry mixture into eight 5-ounce paper cups. Spoon a layer of whipped cream mixture over cranberry mixture; repeat layers. Freeze until firm.

To serve, peel away paper cups and invert onto serving plates. Garnish each serving with a dollop of whipped cream and fresh cranberries.
Yield: 8 servings

Frosty Cranberry Tiptops bring a taste of North America to the meal.

TZIMMES

- 1 pound sweet potatoes, peeled and cut into ½-inch cubes
- 1 pound carrots, thinly sliced
- 2 cups chopped onions
- 2 ribs celery, chopped
- 1 cup chopped pitted prunes (about 6 ounces)
- ½ cup water
- ¼ cup honey
- 2 tablespoons freshly squeezed lemon juice
- 2 teaspoons salt
- 1 teaspoon ground cinnamon
- ½ teaspoon dried lemon peel
- ½ teaspoon ground nutmeg
- ¼ teaspoon ground cloves

Preheat oven to 325 degrees. Place potatoes, carrots, onions, celery, and prunes in a greased 9 x 13-inch baking dish. In a small bowl, combine water, honey, lemon juice, salt, cinnamon, lemon peel, nutmeg, and cloves. Pour honey mixture over vegetables. Cover and bake 1 hour 20 minutes to 1 hour 30 minutes or until potatoes and carrots are tender. Serve hot.
Yield: 10 to 12 servings

CHALLAH

For a non-dairy bread, use water and oil.

- 2 cups milk **or** water
- ½ cup butter or margarine **or** ⅓ cup vegetable oil
- ⅓ cup sugar
- 2 packages dry yeast
- 3 eggs
- 8 cups all-purpose flour
- 2 teaspoons salt
  Vegetable cooking spray
- 1 egg
- 2 teaspoons poppy seed

In a medium saucepan, combine milk, butter, and sugar; heat to 110 degrees. Remove from heat. Stir in yeast and cool 10 minutes.

These traditional Jewish dishes are sure to become family favorites. A braided loaf of Challah, a light, crusty bread, is sprinkled with poppy seeds. Spiced with cinnamon, nutmeg, and cloves, Tzimmes is a medley of sweet potatoes, onions, carrots, celery, and prunes.

Pour milk mixture into a large bowl. Add 3 eggs; beat until well blended. Add flour and salt; stir until a soft dough forms. Turn onto a lightly floured surface and knead until dough becomes smooth and elastic. Place in a large bowl sprayed with cooking spray, turning once to coat top of dough. Cover and let rise in a warm place (80 to 85 degrees) 1 hour or until doubled in size.

Turn dough onto a lightly floured surface and punch down. Divide dough in half. Use a floured rolling pin to roll each half into a 9 x 13-inch rectangle. Cut each rectangle lengthwise into 3 equal strips. For each loaf, braid 3 strips of dough together; transfer to a separate baking sheet sprayed with cooking spray. Spray tops of loaves with cooking spray. Let rise in a warm place 1 hour or until doubled in size.

Preheat oven to 350 degrees. In a small bowl, beat 1 egg. Brush loaves with egg. Sprinkle poppy seed evenly over both loaves. Bake 25 to 30 minutes or until golden brown and bread sounds hollow when tapped. Serve warm.
Yield: 2 loaves bread

GREEN BEAN SAUTÉ

- 1/4 cup butter or margarine
- 1 pound fresh mushrooms, sliced
- 1/2 cup finely chopped onion
- 2 cloves garlic, minced
- 1 teaspoon salt
- 1/2 teaspoon ground black pepper
- 2 cans (16 ounces each) cut green beans, drained
- 1 cup (7 ounces) crumbled feta cheese

In a large skillet, melt butter over medium heat. Add mushrooms, onion, garlic, salt, and pepper; cook until mushrooms are tender. Add green beans; cook 5 to 7 minutes or until heated through. Stir in cheese. Serve hot.
Yield: about 10 servings

TORTILLA SOUP

- 6 cans (14 1/2 ounces each) chicken broth
- 2 cans (4 1/2 ounces each) chopped mild green chiles, undrained
- 1/3 cup fresh mint leaves
- 2 cloves garlic, minced
- 1 teaspoon chili powder
- 1 teaspoon ground cumin
- 1 cup chopped fresh tomatoes
- 2 avocados, peeled, pitted, and chopped
- 1/2 cup chopped fresh cilantro
- 4 slices bacon, cooked and crumbled
- 3 cups coarsely crushed tortilla chips
  Sour cream and fresh cilantro to garnish

For soup, combine chicken broth, chiles, mint leaves, garlic, chili powder, and cumin in a Dutch oven. Bring to a boil. Reduce heat to medium, cover, and simmer 1 hour.

While broth is simmering, combine tomatoes, avocados, chopped cilantro, and bacon in a medium bowl; set aside. Strain broth and return to pan; bring to a boil again.

Chunks of fresh tomato and avocado lend festive color to Mexican Tortilla Soup. Feta cheese, garlic, and fresh mushrooms make our Greek Green Bean Sauté especially savory.

To serve, spoon about 1/4 cup each of avocado mixture and tortilla chips into each bowl. Ladle broth into each bowl. Garnish with sour cream and cilantro. Serve immediately.
Yield: about 12 servings

English Christmas Cabbage is simmered in beef broth and lightly sweetened with brown sugar. Pork-fried rice is molded in a ring shape and paired with a spicy mixture of broccoli and onions seasoned with red peppers to create the Chinese Rice Ring with Broccoli.

CHINESE RICE RING WITH BROCCOLI

RICE

Vegetable cooking spray
1 egg, beaten
2 tablespoons vegetable oil
1/2 cup diced uncooked pork
1/2 cup finely chopped fresh
 mushrooms
1/2 cup finely chopped green onions
4 cups cooked white rice
1/2 cup drained canned green peas
1/4 cup soy sauce

BROCCOLI FILLING

1/8 cup sesame oil
3 dried whole red peppers
2 tablespoons soy sauce
2 tablespoons rice wine vinegar
1 tablespoon sugar
1 teaspoon garlic powder
1/2 teaspoon ground ginger
8 cups fresh broccoli flowerets
1 onion, thinly sliced

For rice, spray a small skillet with cooking spray. Add egg and cook, without stirring, until firm. Place cooked egg on a cutting board and finely chop. In a large skillet, heat oil over medium-high heat. Add pork, mushrooms, and green onions. Stirring constantly, cook 4 to 5 minutes or until pork is cooked. Stir in rice, peas, chopped egg, and soy sauce. Pack hot rice mixture into a

112

6-cup ring mold sprayed with cooking spray. Cover and place in a 200-degree oven until ready to serve.

For broccoli filling, combine sesame oil and red peppers in a large skillet. Cook over medium heat 3 to 4 minutes. Stir in soy sauce, vinegar, sugar, garlic powder, and ginger. Add broccoli and onion, stirring to coat well. Stirring occasionally, cook until broccoli is tender. Remove from heat; remove peppers. Invert rice ring onto a serving plate and spoon broccoli into center of ring. Serve hot.

Yield: about 12 servings

ENGLISH CHRISTMAS CABBAGE

1/2   pound bacon
2   cans (14 1/2 ounces each) beef broth
1/2   cup firmly packed brown sugar
1/4   cup apple cider vinegar
2   teaspoons salt
1   teaspoon ground black pepper
3   pounds red cabbage, shredded

In a Dutch oven, cook bacon over medium-high heat until crisp. Reserving drippings, remove bacon from pan; crumble and set aside. Add beef broth, brown sugar, vinegar, salt, and pepper to bacon drippings in Dutch oven. Cook over medium-high heat, stirring until sugar dissolves and mixture comes to a boil. Add cabbage and bring to a boil. Reduce heat to medium-low, cover, and simmer 30 minutes. Transfer to a serving bowl; sprinkle crumbled bacon over cabbage. Serve hot.

Yield: about 16 servings

CHOCOLATE-RASPBERRY CAKE

1   package (18.25 ounces) devil's food cake mix
1 1/4   cups water
3   eggs
1/3   cup vegetable oil

1   jar (12 ounces) seedless raspberry jam
1   can (16 ounces) chocolate-flavored ready-to-spread frosting
   Sliced almonds to garnish

Preheat oven to 350 degrees. Line bottoms of 3 lightly greased 9-inch round cake pans with waxed paper. Combine cake mix, water, eggs, and oil in a large bowl; beat at low speed of an electric mixer 30 seconds. Beat at medium speed 2 minutes. Pour batter evenly into prepared pans. Bake 15 to 18 minutes or until a toothpick inserted in center of cake comes out clean. Cool in pans 5 minutes. Remove from pans and cool completely on a wire rack.

To assemble cake, melt raspberry jam in a medium saucepan over medium heat; remove from heat. Place 1 cake layer on a serving plate. Brush a thin layer of melted jam over layer and spread frosting over jam. Repeat with second layer. Place third layer on top. Spread sides of cake with remaining frosting; bring frosting up around edge of cake top to form a small ridge. Spread remaining melted jam over top of cake. Garnish with almond slices. Store in an airtight container.

Yield: about 16 servings

For a heavenly finale, serve velvety Chocolate-Raspberry Cake topped with jam and crowned with almonds.

113

114

MOUSSE AU CHOCOLATE

- 3/4 cup butter or margarine, cut into pieces
- 1 cup whipping cream, divided
- 5 eggs, separated
- 1 package (6 ounces) semisweet chocolate chips
- 1/4 cup orange-flavored liqueur
- 2/3 cup granulated sugar
- 2 tablespoons water
- 1/4 teaspoon cream of tartar
- 1/2 cup sifted confectioners sugar
- 1 teaspoon orange extract
  Mandarin oranges, well drained, to garnish

Combine butter, 1/4 cup whipping cream, and egg yolks in top of a double boiler. Whisking constantly, cook over simmering water until mixture reaches 160 degrees on a thermometer (about 10 minutes). Remove from heat and stir in chocolate chips; stir until smooth. Transfer to a a small bowl and cool to room temperature. Stir in liqueur.

Combine egg whites, granulated sugar, water, and cream of tartar in top of double boiler. Whisking constantly, cook over simmering water until mixture reaches 160 degrees (about 9 minutes). Transfer to a large bowl and beat until stiff peaks form. Gently fold chocolate mixture into egg white mixture. Spoon mousse into small serving dishes, loosely cover, and chill until ready to serve.

Place a medium bowl and beaters from an electric mixer in freezer until well chilled. In chilled bowl, whip remaining 3/4 cup whipping cream until soft peaks form. Add confectioners sugar and orange extract; beat until stiff peaks form. Garnish with whipped cream and mandarin oranges.

Yield: about 8 servings

Guests will love these after-dinner treats! From France, Mousse au Chocolate combines orange and chocolate flavors. African Benne Seed Cookies are thin, sweet sesame seed wafers, and Jamaican Chocolate Rum Balls are rich and moist.

BENNE SEED COOKIES

- 1 cup (about 5 ounces) sesame seed
- 1/4 cup butter or margarine, softened
- 1 cup sugar
- 1 egg
- 1 teaspoon freshly squeezed lemon juice
- 1 teaspoon vanilla extract
- 1/2 cup all-purpose flour
- 1/4 teaspoon salt
- 1/4 teaspoon baking powder

Preheat oven to 350 degrees. Spread sesame seed on an ungreased baking sheet. Stirring occasionally, bake 5 to 8 minutes or until golden brown. Cool completely on pan.

In a medium bowl, cream butter and sugar until fluffy. Add egg, lemon juice, and vanilla; stir until well blended. In a small bowl, combine flour, salt, and baking powder. Add dry ingredients to creamed mixture and stir until a soft dough forms. Stir in sesame seed. Drop teaspoonfuls of dough 1 inch apart onto a heavily greased baking sheet. Bake 6 to 8 minutes or until edges are lightly browned. Transfer to a wire rack to cool completely. Store in an airtight container.

Yield: about 5 dozen cookies

CHOCOLATE RUM BALLS

- 1 package (12 ounces) semisweet chocolate chips, divided
- 1/4 cup sour cream
- 1 tablespoon honey
- 1/4 teaspoon salt
- 1 3/4 cups graham cracker crumbs
- 1 cup sifted confectioners sugar
- 3/4 cup ground walnuts
- 1/2 cup butter or margarine, melted
- 1/3 cup rum

Combine 1 cup chocolate chips, sour cream, honey, and salt in a small saucepan. Stirring constantly, cook over low heat until smooth. Pour into an 8-inch square pan, cover, and freeze 20 minutes. Shape teaspoonfuls of chocolate mixture into about 36 balls; place on aluminum foil and freeze 10 minutes.

Process remaining 1 cup chocolate chips in a food processor until finely ground; transfer to a small bowl and set aside. In a large bowl, combine cracker crumbs, confectioners sugar, walnuts, butter, and rum. Press crumb mixture around each chocolate ball, forming 1 1/2-inch balls. Immediately roll in ground chocolate. Store in an airtight container in refrigerator. Serve chilled.

Yield: about 3 dozen rum balls

DELIGHTFUL DESSERTS

Whether you need a grand finale for a special dinner or a selection of treats to serve with coffee, you'll find a delectable solution in this enticing collection of desserts! Family and friends will savor the old-fashioned pies and cakes, extravagant tortes, and rich, creamy cheesecakes. This luscious array of goodies is sure to sweeten the mood of an already jubilant occasion!

With its elegant gold bow, this yummy Almond Cake (recipe on page 118) would look right at home under the Christmas tree! Packed with toasted almonds, the layered cake is light and fluffy. Almond extract lends extra flavor to the creamy frosting.

ALMOND CAKE

(Shown on pages 116 and 117)

CAKE

- 1 cup whole unsalted almonds
- 1 cup butter or margarine, softened
- 2 cups sugar
- 5 eggs
- 1 teaspoon vanilla extract
- 1 teaspoon almond extract
- 2 cups all-purpose flour
- 1 teaspoon baking soda
- 1/2 teaspoon salt
- 1 cup buttermilk

FROSTING

- 6 3/4 cups sifted confectioners sugar
- 2 cups butter or margarine, softened
- 7 tablespoons milk
- 1 teaspoon almond extract
  Ribbon to decorate

Preheat oven to 350 degrees. To toast almonds, spread on an ungreased baking sheet. Bake 5 to 8 minutes or until almonds are slightly darker in color. Cool completely on baking sheet. Finely chop almonds; set aside.

For cake, cream butter and sugar in a large bowl until fluffy. Add eggs, 1 at a time, beating well after each addition. Stir in extracts. Sift flour, baking soda, and salt into a medium bowl. Stir dry ingredients and buttermilk alternately into creamed mixture. Stir in almonds. Pour batter into 2 greased and floured 8-inch square baking pans. Bake 30 to 35 minutes or until a toothpick inserted in center of cake comes out clean. Cool in pans 10 minutes. Remove from pans and cool completely on a wire rack.

For frosting, combine confectioners sugar, butter, milk, and almond extract in a large bowl; beat until smooth. Spread frosting between layers and on sides and top of cake. Decorate with ribbon. Store in an airtight container in refrigerator. Remove ribbon before serving.

Yield: about 20 servings

AMARETTO TRUFFLES

Keep a tin of these truffles in your refrigerator as a special treat to serve drop-in guests.

- 2 egg yolks
- 4 tablespoons whipping cream
- 1 package (12 ounces) semisweet chocolate chips
- 1/2 cup butter or margarine, softened
- 3 tablespoons cream cheese
- 1/3 cup amaretto
- 1 cup slivered almonds, toasted and finely chopped
  Amaretto and sweetened whipped cream to serve

Whisking constantly, cook egg yolks and whipping cream in top of a double boiler until mixture reaches 160 degrees on a thermometer (about 15 minutes). Transfer egg mixture to a small bowl and set aside. Melt chocolate chips in top of a double boiler over low heat. Remove from heat and stir in butter, 1 tablespoon at a time. Beat egg yolk mixture into chocolate mixture (mixture will begin to thicken). Beat cream cheese and 1/3 cup amaretto into chocolate mixture until smooth. Cover and chill until firm.

Shape mixture into 1 1/2-inch balls. Roll in almonds. Cover and chill.

To serve, pour about 2 tablespoons amaretto into a wine glass. Place 1 truffle in glass and top with whipped cream.

Yield: about 30 truffles

For an elegant dessert, serve Amaretto Truffles in a glass with liqueur and whipped cream.

This attractive Cream Puff Ring gets its delicate flavor from the orange liqueur in its custard filling and chocolate glaze.

CREAM PUFF RING

PASTRY
- 1 cup water
- 1/2 cup butter or margarine
- 1 cup all-purpose flour
- 1/8 teaspoon salt
- 4 eggs

PASTRY CREAM
- 3 egg yolks
- 1/2 cup sugar
- 2 tablespoons all-purpose flour
- 3/4 cup milk
- 1/4 cup orange-flavored liqueur
- 1 cup whipping cream, whipped

GLAZE
- 2 ounces unsweetened baking chocolate
- 1 tablespoon butter or margarine
- 2 cups sifted confectioners sugar
- 1/4 cup boiling water
- 2 tablespoons orange-flavored liqueur

Preheat oven to 400 degrees. For pastry, combine water and butter in a medium saucepan over medium heat. Cook until butter melts. Stir in flour and salt until well blended. Stirring constantly, cook over medium heat until mixture forms a ball. Remove from heat; cool 10 minutes. Add eggs, 1 at a time, beating well after each addition. Line a 9-inch round cake pan with aluminum foil. Drop eight 1/4 cupfuls of dough in pan 1/2 inch apart, forming a circle. Bake 30 minutes. Reduce oven to 375 degrees; bake pastries 20 minutes longer. Cut slits in ring to allow steam to escape. Continue baking 20 minutes longer. Remove from pan; cool on foil.

For pastry cream, beat egg yolks and sugar until mixture is light in color. Stir in flour and milk. Transfer mixture to a heavy large saucepan. Stirring constantly, bring to a boil over medium heat. Cook until very thick (about 4 minutes). Remove from heat and stir in liqueur; cool completely, stirring occasionally. Fold in whipped cream.

For glaze, melt chocolate and butter in top of a double boiler. Remove from heat and beat in confectioners sugar, water, and liqueur; set aside. Carefully slice tops from pastries. Pull soft dough from insides. Fill with pastry cream. Replace tops and spoon glaze over ring.
Yield: 8 servings

CHOCOLATE-ORANGE CUSTARDS

CUSTARDS

        5   egg yolks
      1/3   cup sugar
        1   package (6 ounces) semisweet
              chocolate chips, melted
     1 1/2 cups whipping cream
      1/4   cup milk
        1   tablespoon orange-flavored
              liqueur
        1   teaspoon dried orange peel

TOPPING

      1/2   cup whipping cream
        1   tablespoon sugar
      1/2   teaspoon dried orange peel
      1/8   cup semisweet chocolate chips,
              finely ground
        1   tablespoon orange-flavored
              liqueur

Preheat oven to 325 degrees. For custards, beat egg yolks and sugar in a medium bowl until well blended using an electric mixer. Add melted chocolate; beat until well blended. Beat in whipping cream, milk, liqueur, and orange peel. Place 12 small ramekins (or twenty-four 2-inch foil baking cups) in 9 x 13-inch baking pans. Fill each ramekin with custard mixture. Fill pans with hot water to come halfway up sides of ramekins. Bake 1 hour to 1 hour 15 minutes or until a knife inserted near center of custard comes out clean. Cool completely in pans of water. Remove ramekins from pans, cover, and refrigerate until well chilled.

For topping, place a medium bowl and beaters from an electric mixer in refrigerator until well chilled. In chilled bowl, combine whipping cream, sugar, and orange peel; whip until stiff peaks form. Fold in chocolate chips and liqueur. Spoon about 1 tablespoon topping over each chilled custard. Store in an airtight container in refrigerator until ready to serve.

Yield: 1 dozen ramekins or 2 dozen baking cups custard

Rich Chocolate-Orange Custards are garnished with sweetened whipped cream that's also flavored with orange and chocolate. Brandy adds warmth to cranberry and orange juices in Cranberry-Brandy Punch, and Jam Cake Squares feature strawberry preserves layered between a buttery crust and an apple-flavored topping.

CRANBERRY-BRANDY PUNCH

        5   cups cranberry juice cocktail
        3   cups orange juice
        2   cups brandy

To serve warm, combine all ingredients in a large saucepan or Dutch oven. Cook over medium heat until heated through. Serve immediately.

To serve chilled, combine all ingredients in a 3-quart container. Serve over ice.

Yield: about 10 cups punch

JAM CAKE SQUARES

CRUST
- 1 cup all-purpose flour
- 3 tablespoons sifted confectioners sugar
- 1/4 teaspoon salt
- 1/2 cup chilled butter or margarine, cut into small pieces

TOPPING
- 2/3 cup strawberry jam or preserves
- 1 1/4 cups granulated sugar
- 4 tablespoons all-purpose flour
- 1/2 teaspoon baking powder
- 3 eggs
- 1/4 cup applesauce
  Confectioners sugar

Preheat oven to 350 degrees. For crust, combine flour, confectioners sugar, and salt in a medium bowl. Using a pastry blender or 2 knives, cut in butter until mixture resembles coarse meal. Press into bottom of a greased and floured 8 x 11-inch baking pan. Bake 10 minutes.

For topping, spread jam evenly over hot crust. Bake 10 minutes or until jam is bubbly; set aside. In a medium bowl, combine granulated sugar, flour, and baking powder. Add eggs and applesauce; beat until well blended. Spread topping evenly over jam. Bake 30 to 35 minutes or until golden brown and firm in center. Cool completely on a wire rack. Dust with confectioners sugar. Refrigerate until ready to serve. To serve, cut into 2-inch squares.

Yield: about 1 1/2 dozen squares

Moist, chewy Peanut Butter Brownies are made with extra-crunchy peanut butter so they're packed with nutty flavor.

PEANUT BUTTER BROWNIES

- 1/4 cup butter or margarine, melted
- 1/2 cup granulated sugar
- 1/2 cup firmly packed brown sugar
- 2 eggs
- 1 teaspoon vanilla extract
- 1/2 cup all-purpose flour
- 1/2 teaspoon baking powder
- 1/2 teaspoon salt
- 1/2 cup extra-crunchy peanut butter

Preheat oven to 350 degrees. In a medium bowl, combine butter and sugars. Add eggs and vanilla; beat until smooth. In a small bowl, combine flour, baking powder, and salt. Add dry ingredients to creamed mixture; stir just until dry ingredients are moistened. Stir in peanut butter. Spread batter in a greased 8 x 11-inch baking pan. Bake 20 to 25 minutes or until set in center. Cool completely in pan. Cut into 2-inch squares.

Yield: about 1 1/2 dozen brownies

Mellow pears and tart apples are a delicious combination in this Apple-Pear Tart. A creamy filling is hidden beneath the wine-glazed fruit, and the flaky crust has a hint of orange juice.

APPLE-PEAR TART

CRUST
- 1/3 cup butter or margarine, softened
- 1/4 cup sugar
- 1 egg yolk
- 1 tablespoon frozen orange juice concentrate, thawed
- 1/2 teaspoon vanilla extract
- 1 cup all-purpose flour
- 1/3 cup graham cracker crumbs

FILLING
- 2/3 cup sugar
- 1/4 cup cornstarch
- 2 2/3 cups whipping cream
- 2 eggs, beaten
- 1 teaspoon vanilla extract

TOPPING
- 4 teaspoons cornstarch
- 1 tablespoon water

- 2/3 cup dry red wine
- 1/2 cup sugar
- 2 cups peeled, cored, and chopped Granny Smith apples (about 2 medium apples)
- 3 very ripe pears

Preheat oven to 350 degrees. For crust, cream butter and sugar in a

122

medium bowl until fluffy. Add egg yolk, orange juice, and vanilla; beat until smooth. Add flour and cracker crumbs; knead in bowl until a soft dough forms. Press into bottom and up sides of a greased 8 x 11-inch tart pan with a removable bottom. Prick bottom of crust with a fork. Bake 20 minutes or until lightly browned. Cool completely on a wire rack.

For filling, combine sugar and cornstarch in a medium saucepan. Slowly stir in whipping cream and cook over medium heat until mixture begins to simmer. Reduce heat to low and cook 2 to 3 minutes or until filling thickens and coats the back of a spoon. Stir about 1/2 cup whipping cream mixture into eggs. Whisk egg mixture and vanilla into remaining whipping cream mixture in pan. Stirring constantly, cook 3 minutes. Remove from heat and cool to room temperature. Pour into cooled crust.

For topping, combine cornstarch and water in a small bowl; stir to form a paste. In a medium saucepan, combine wine and sugar. Stirring constantly, cook over medium heat until sugar dissolves. Whisk cornstarch mixture into wine mixture. Stir in apples. Bring to a boil and cook 5 to 8 minutes or until thickened. Remove from heat. Using a sharp knife, peel, halve, and core each pear. Beginning at least 1/2 inch from stem end, make lengthwise cuts in each pear half as shown in **Fig. 1**.

Fig. 1

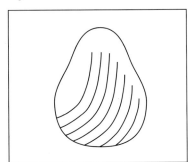

Fan slices and arrange pears on top of filling. Spoon apple mixture evenly over pears. Cover and refrigerate 1 hour or until set. Remove sides of pan to serve.
Yield: about 12 servings

Light and refreshing, Pink Squirrel Pie is flavored with amaretto and crème de menthe. The chewy crust features coconut macaroons and toasted almonds.

PINK SQUIRREL PIE

CRUST

14	coconut macaroons, crushed
1/4	cup finely chopped almonds, toasted
3	tablespoons butter or margarine, melted

FILLING

24	large marshmallows
3/4	cup milk
1/2	cup amaretto
1/2	cup white crème de menthe
2 1/2	teaspoons almond extract
3	to 4 drops red food coloring
2	cups whipping cream, whipped

Preheat oven to 350 degrees. In a medium bowl, combine macaroons, almonds, and butter. Press into bottom and up sides of an ungreased 9-inch pie pan. Bake 10 minutes.

In a heavy large saucepan, melt marshmallows in milk over medium heat; cool. Stir in amaretto, crème de menthe, almond extract, and food coloring. Fold in whipped cream. Pour into pie crust. Cover and freeze 6 to 8 hours or until firm.
Yield: about 8 servings

These little morsels are wonderful treats! Flavored with cinnamon and brandy extract, creamy Chestnut Mousse is served in lacy Chocolate Cups. Flaky Coconut-Chocolate Turnovers feature a sweet filling of coconut and chocolate chips.

124

CHESTNUT MOUSSE IN CHOCOLATE CUPS

Chocolate cups may be made in advance and stored in the freezer or refrigerator.

CHOCOLATE CUPS
- 1 package (12 ounces) semisweet chocolate chips
- 2 teaspoons butter-flavored shortening

CHESTNUT MOUSSE
- 1 envelope unflavored gelatin
- 1/4 cup cold water
- 1 can (17.5 ounces) chestnut spread (available at gourmet food stores)
- 1 cup sugar, divided
- 1 teaspoon vanilla extract
- 1 teaspoon imitation brandy extract
- 1 teaspoon ground cinnamon
- 1 cup whipping cream
  Cocoa to garnish

For chocolate cups, invert 12 foil baking cups on waxed paper. Stirring constantly, melt chocolate chips and shortening in a medium saucepan over low heat. Remove from heat; cool slightly. Spoon chocolate mixture into a pastry bag fitted with a small round tip. Pipe chocolate mixture randomly over bottom and sides of each cup, making sure piped lines overlap. If necessary, smooth chocolate on bottom of each cup with a knife so cup will sit level. Freeze 30 minutes or until firm. Carefully peel away baking cups.

For chestnut mousse, place a large bowl and beaters from an electric mixer in refrigerator until well chilled. In a small saucepan, sprinkle gelatin over water; allow to stand 1 minute. Stirring constantly, cook gelatin over low heat until gelatin dissolves. In a large bowl, combine chestnut spread and 1/2 cup sugar until well blended. Add gelatin mixture, vanilla, brandy extract, and cinnamon to chestnut mixture; beat until well blended. In chilled bowl, beat whipping cream until soft peaks form. Gradually add remaining 1/2 cup sugar; beat until stiff peaks form. Fold whipped cream into chestnut mixture. Spoon about 1/3 cup mousse into each chocolate cup. Dust lightly with cocoa. Cover and refrigerate until ready to serve.

Yield: about 12 servings

COCONUT-CHOCOLATE TURNOVERS

- 1 egg white
- 1 cup sweetened shredded coconut
- 1/4 cup sugar
- 2 tablespoons light corn syrup
- 1/8 teaspoon salt
- 1 teaspoon coconut extract
- 1 package (17 1/4 ounces) frozen puff pastry, thawed
- 1/2 cup semisweet chocolate chips

In a small bowl, whisk egg white until foamy. In a medium saucepan, combine coconut, sugar, corn syrup, and salt. Stirring constantly, cook over medium-low heat 5 to 6 minutes or until sugar dissolves and mixture thickens. Stirring constantly, add egg white to coconut mixture. Cook 5 to 6 minutes or until mixture becomes stiff and very sticky. Remove from heat and stir in coconut extract. Cool to room temperature.

Preheat oven to 400 degrees. On a lightly floured surface, cut pastry sheets into 3-inch squares. Place about 1 teaspoon chocolate chips in center of each square. Spoon about 1 tablespoon coconut mixture over chocolate chips. Fold dough over each filling to form a triangle; use a fork to crimp edges together. Turn pastries over and crimp edges again. Transfer to an ungreased baking sheet. Bake 15 to 20 minutes or until puffed and golden brown. Cool completely on a wire rack.

Yield: 1 1/2 dozen turnovers

This yummy chocolate Tunnel Cake has a double surprise inside — a rich cream cheese filling loaded with miniature chocolate chips!

TUNNEL CAKE

FILLING
- 11 ounces cream cheese, softened
- 1/3 cup sugar
- 1 egg
- 1 cup semisweet chocolate mini chips

CAKE
- 3 cups all-purpose flour
- 2 cups sugar
- 1/2 cup cocoa
- 2 teaspoons baking soda
- 1 teaspoon salt
- 2 cups water
- 2/3 cup vegetable oil
- 2 tablespoons white vinegar
- 1 tablespoon vanilla extract

Preheat oven to 350 degrees. For filling, combine cream cheese, sugar, and egg in a small bowl; beat until well blended. Stir in chocolate chips; set aside.

For cake, combine flour, sugar, cocoa, baking soda, and salt in a large bowl. Add water, oil, vinegar, and vanilla; beat until well blended. Pour half of batter into a well-greased 10-inch fluted tube pan. Spread filling over batter; top with remaining batter. Bake 50 to 55 minutes or until toothpick inserted in center of cake comes out clean. Cool in pan 10 minutes. Remove cake from pan and cool on a wire rack.

Yield: about 16 servings

Richest Chocolate Cake is a delectable blend of dark chocolate and coffee-flavored liqueur. It's topped with a chocolate frosting and garnished with walnut halves.

RICHEST CHOCOLATE CAKE

CAKE
1¹/₂ cups all-purpose flour
1¹/₄ cups sugar
3 tablespoons cocoa
1 tablespoon baking soda
¹/₂ teaspoon salt
4 eggs
¹/₂ cup milk

¹/₂ cup coffee-flavored liqueur
¹/₃ cup vegetable oil
1 tablespoon white vinegar
1 teaspoon vanilla extract
2 packages (3 ounces each) cream cheese, softened
1 package (6 ounces) semisweet chocolate chips, melted

FROSTING
2 ounces unsweetened baking chocolate
2 tablespoons butter or margarine
1¹/₂ cups sifted confectioners sugar
1 teaspoon vanilla extract
3 tablespoons plus 1 teaspoon hot water
Walnut halves to garnish

Preheat oven to 350 degrees. For cake, line bottom of a 9-inch springform tube pan with waxed paper. Grease and flour waxed paper and sides of pan; set aside. In a large bowl, combine flour, sugar, cocoa, baking soda, and salt. In a medium bowl, whisk eggs, milk, liqueur, oil, vinegar, and vanilla. Add egg mixture to dry ingredients; stir until well blended. In a medium bowl, combine cream cheese and melted chocolate until well blended. Beat cream cheese mixture into batter. Pour batter into prepared pan. Bake 45 to 50 minutes or until a toothpick inserted in center of cake comes out clean. Cool in pan 10 minutes; remove sides of pan and cool completely. Invert onto a serving plate; remove waxed paper.

For frosting, melt chocolate and butter in a small saucepan over low heat, stirring constantly. Remove from heat; add sugar and vanilla. Stir until crumbly. Add water and stir until smooth. Spread frosting over cake. Garnish with walnuts.
Yield: about 16 servings

COCONUT CREAM

This old-fashioned dessert is a snap to make during the busy holiday season. We decorated the mold with artificial greenery and shiny candy dragées.

3	envelopes unflavored gelatin
1/3	cup cold water
5	cups whipping cream, divided
1	cup sugar
1 1/2	teaspoons coconut extract
2	cups flaked coconut

In a small bowl, sprinkle gelatin over water; allow to stand one minute. In a heavy medium saucepan, bring 2 cups whipping cream to a boil over medium heat. Add gelatin mixture and sugar. Stirring constantly, cook until sugar dissolves; cool.

Beat remaining 3 cups whipping cream and coconut extract until soft peaks form. Fold whipped cream mixture and coconut into gelatin mixture. Pour into a lightly oiled 8-cup mold. Chill 6 to 8 hours or until firm.
Yield: 8 to 10 servings

Our light and fluffy Coconut Cream mold is an elegant dessert that can be prepared ahead of time.

Baked in a chocolate cookie crumb crust and topped with chocolate, caramel, and nuts, Turtle Cheesecake is a luscious dessert.

TURTLE CHEESECAKE

Turtle Cheesecake may be made one day in advance.

CRUST
1 package (9 ounces) chocolate wafer cookies
¼ cup sugar
6 tablespoons butter or margarine, melted

FILLING
3 packages (8 ounces each) cream cheese, softened
1¼ cups sugar
4 eggs
1 cup sour cream
1 tablespoon vanilla extract

TOPPING
1 package (6 ounces) semisweet chocolate chips

¼ cup butter or margarine
1 jar (12½ ounces) caramel topping
1 cup chopped pecans

DECORATIVE CHOCOLATE ICING
1 cup sifted confectioners sugar
½ cup butter or margarine, softened
¼ cup cocoa
1 tablespoon milk

Preheat oven to 350 degrees. For crust, process cookies in a food processor until finely ground. Add sugar and butter; process until mixture resembles fine meal. Press into bottom and 1 inch up sides of a greased 9-inch springform pan. Bake 10 minutes. Cool completely on a wire rack.

For filling, beat cream cheese in a large bowl until smooth using an electric mixer. Add sugar and eggs; beat until fluffy. Add sour cream and vanilla; beat until well blended. Pour filling into crust. Bake 1 hour to 1 hour 10 minutes or until set in center. Turn off oven. Leaving door slightly open, leave cheesecake in oven 1 hour. Cool completely on a wire rack. Remove sides of pan.

For topping, melt chocolate chips and butter in a small saucepan over low heat, stirring constantly. Spread chocolate evenly over top of cooled cake. Cool completely. In a medium saucepan, combine caramel topping and pecans. Stirring constantly, bring mixture to a boil over medium heat and cook 2 to 3 minutes or until thickened. Remove from heat; cool 5 minutes. Spread caramel mixture evenly over chocolate. Cool completely.

For decorative chocolate icing, combine confectioners sugar, butter, cocoa, and milk in a medium bowl; beat until smooth using an electric mixer. Spoon icing into a pastry bag fitted with a large star tip. Pipe a decorative border along top edge of cake. Cover and refrigerate 8 hours or overnight before serving.
Yield: about 16 servings

WHITE CHOCOLATE MOUSSE

10 ounces white baking chocolate, cut into pieces
1/4 cup whipping cream
6 eggs, separated
1 cup sifted confectioners sugar, divided
1/2 cup hazelnut liqueur

Creamy White Chocolate Mousse is a tantalizing taste treat that few can resist.

2 tablespoons water
3/4 teaspoon cream of tartar
2 cups whipping cream, whipped
Grated semisweet chocolate and a maraschino cherry to garnish

Melt white chocolate and 1/4 cup whipping cream in top of a double boiler over hot water. Set aside to cool slightly.

Beat egg yolks, 1/4 cup confectioners sugar, and liqueur until mixture lightens in color. Stirring constantly, cook mixture in top of double boiler over simmering water until very thick and mixture reaches 160 degrees on a thermometer (about 5 minutes).

Transfer egg mixture to a large bowl. Fold in white chocolate mixture; stir until smooth.

Combine egg whites, remaining 3/4 cup confectioners sugar, water, and cream of tartar in top of double boiler. Whisking constantly, cook over simmering water until mixture reaches 160 degrees. Transfer to a large bowl and beat until stiff peaks form. Gently fold whipped cream into chocolate mixture; then fold in egg white mixture. Cover and refrigerate until set.

To serve, garnish with grated chocolate and cherry.
Yield: 10 to 12 servings

Slices of Raspberry Pound Cake are garnished with two kinds of chocolate, sprinkled with pistachios, and served with a tangy raspberry sauce.

RASPBERRY POUND CAKE

RASPBERRY SAUCE
- 2 packages (16 ounces each) frozen red raspberries, thawed
- 2 tablespoons sifted confectioners sugar
- 2 teaspoons cornstarch
- 2 tablespoons raspberry-flavored liqueur

CAKE
- 1 package (16 ounces) pound cake mix
- 2/3 cup water
- 2 eggs
- 1/4 teaspoon raspberry-flavored oil (used in candy making)
  Pink paste food coloring

TOPPING
- 1/2 cup semisweet chocolate chips
- 2 tablespoons butter or margarine
- 1 ounce white baking chocolate, chopped
- 1/2 cup chopped pistachios

For raspberry sauce, process raspberries in a food processor until puréed. Strain; discard seeds and pulp. Place raspberry juice, confectioners sugar, and cornstarch in a small saucepan. Stirring constantly, bring to a boil over medium heat. Boil 1 minute. Remove from heat. Stir in liqueur. Cover and refrigerate until well chilled.

Preheat oven to 325 degrees. For cake, combine cake mix, water, eggs, and raspberry-flavored oil in a large bowl. Mix according to cake mix instructions. Tint batter pink. Spoon batter into a greased and floured 5 x 9-inch loaf pan. Bake 55 to 60 minutes or until a toothpick

inserted in center of cake comes out clean. Cool in pan 10 minutes. Remove from pan and cool completely on a wire rack.

For topping, melt chocolate chips and butter in a small saucepan over low heat, stirring constantly. Remove from heat. Place white chocolate in a disposable plastic pastry bag and microwave on medium power (50%) at 30 second intervals until melted. Spoon about 2 tablespoons raspberry sauce onto each serving plate. Cut cake into 1/2-inch slices. Place 1 slice cake over sauce. Spread a thin layer of semisweet chocolate mixture diagonally over half of each slice. Cut tip of pastry bag to create a small hole and pipe white chocolate over each slice of cake. Sprinkle with pistachios.

Yield: about 16 servings

Individual Chocolate-Carrot Cakes are an innovative variation of the traditional recipe. Filled with carrots, nuts, and chocolate chips, the moist cakes are topped with an incredible chocolate-cream cheese frosting. Rich, creamy Mocha-Cardamom Cappuccino is laced with rum and coffee-flavored liqueur.

CHOCOLATE-CARROT CAKES

CAKES
- ½ cup butter or margarine, softened
- ½ cup vegetable oil
- 1¾ cups sugar
- 2 eggs
- ½ cup buttermilk
- 1 teaspoon vanilla extract
- 2½ cups all-purpose flour
- ¼ cup cocoa
- 1 teaspoon baking soda
- ½ teaspoon salt
- ½ teaspoon ground nutmeg
- 2 cups finely shredded carrots (about 4 medium carrots)
- 1 package (6 ounces) semisweet chocolate chips
- ¾ cup finely chopped walnuts

FROSTING
- 1⅓ cups confectioners sugar, sifted
- 2 packages (3 ounces each) cream cheese, softened
- ⅓ cup butter or margarine, softened
- 2 tablespoons cocoa
- 1 teaspoon vanilla extract
  Red and green candied cherries to garnish

For cakes, preheat oven to 350 degrees. In a large bowl, cream butter, oil, and sugar until fluffy. Add eggs, 1 at a time, beating well after each addition. Add buttermilk and vanilla; beat until smooth. Sift flour, cocoa, baking soda, salt, and nutmeg into a medium bowl. Add dry ingredients to creamed mixture; stir until well blended. Stir in carrots, chocolate chips, and walnuts. Pour batter into greased and floured 2¼ x 4-inch loaf pans, filling each pan three-fourths full. Bake 25 to 30 minutes or until sides of cakes begin to pull away from pans and tops spring back when lightly pressed. Cool in pans 10 minutes. Remove from pans and cool completely on a wire rack.

For frosting, beat confectioners sugar, cream cheese, butter, cocoa, and vanilla in a medium bowl until smooth using an electric mixer. Spread frosting on top of each cake. Garnish with candied cherries.
Yield: about 1½ dozen cakes

MOCHA-CARDAMOM CAPPUCCINO

- 3 cups brewed coffee
- 3 cups half and half
- 1 cup rum
- 1 cup coffee-flavored liqueur
- 2 teaspoons ground cardamom

In a large saucepan or Dutch oven, combine coffee, half and half, rum, liqueur, and cardamom. Cook over medium heat until mixture begins to boil. Remove from heat. Serve immediately.
Yield: about 7½ cups cappuccino

Luscious dark berries gleam like polished gemstones atop this moist Blueberries and Cream Cheesecake. A pleasing blend of Burgundy, brandy, and cranberry juice, Cranberry Sangria is garnished with colorful fruit kabobs.

BLUEBERRIES AND CREAM CHEESECAKE

CRUST

1 package (12 ounces) vanilla wafer cookies, finely crushed
3/4 cup butter or margarine, melted

FILLING

5 packages (8 ounces each) cream cheese, softened
1 1/2 cups sugar
6 eggs
2 egg yolks
3 tablespoons all-purpose flour
3 teaspoons vanilla extract
1/4 cup whipping cream

TOPPING

3 tablespoons cornstarch
1 cup plus 3 tablespoons water, divided
1 cup sugar
1 package (16 ounces) frozen unsweetened blueberries, thawed and drained

For crust, combine cookie crumbs and butter. Press into bottom and halfway up sides of a greased 9-inch springform pan. Cover and refrigerate.

For filling, beat cream cheese 25 minutes in a large bowl, adding 1 package at a time. Add sugar and beat 5 minutes longer. Add eggs and egg yolks, 1 at a time, beating 2 minutes after each addition. Beat in flour and vanilla. Beat in whipping cream. Preheat oven to 500 degrees. Pour filling into crust. Bake 10 minutes. Reduce heat to 200 degrees. Bake 1 hour. Turn oven off and leave cake in oven 1 hour without opening door. Cool completely on a wire rack. Remove sides of pan.

132

For topping, combine cornstarch and 3 tablespoons water in a small bowl; stir until smooth. Combine sugar and remaining 1 cup water in a small saucepan. Stirring constantly, cook over medium heat until sugar dissolves. Stirring constantly, add cornstarch mixture and cook until mixture boils and thickens. Remove from heat and cool to room temperature. Stir in blueberries. Spoon topping over cheesecake. Loosely cover and refrigerate 8 hours or overnight. Serve chilled.
Yield: about 16 servings

CRANBERRY SANGRIA

1   bottle (750 ml) Burgundy wine
3   cups cranberry juice cocktail
1/4   cup brandy
1/4   cup sugar
1   can (8 ounces) pineapple chunks, drained
1   orange, thinly sliced
     Maraschino cherries
     Wooden skewers

Combine wine, cranberry juice, brandy, and sugar in a 2-quart container. Stir until sugar dissolves. Cover and refrigerate until ready to serve. Add ice and pour sangria into glasses. Place pieces of fruit on wooden skewers; place in glasses.
Yield: about 6 cups sangria

A rich chocolate treat filled with marshmallows and almonds, Rocky Road Mousse is a new twist on a childhood favorite.

ROCKY ROAD MOUSSE

This mousse is a wonderful adult version of the classic treat. It makes plenty for a hungry crowd!

4   eggs, separated
1/2   cup brewed coffee
1   teaspoon vanilla extract
3   cups semisweet chocolate chips
3/4   cup sugar, divided
1   tablespoon water
1/4   teaspoon cream of tartar
1/8   teaspoon salt
1   cup whipping cream
1 1/2   cups miniature marshmallows
1   cup sliced almonds, toasted

In top of a double boiler, combine egg yolks, coffee, and vanilla. Whisking constantly, cook over simmering water until mixture reaches 160 degrees on a thermometer (about 8 to 10 minutes). Gradually stir in chocolate chips, whisking until smooth. Transfer to a large bowl. In top of a double boiler, combine egg whites, 1/2 cup sugar, water, cream of tartar, and salt. Whisking constantly, cook over simmering water until mixture reaches 160 degrees (about 10 to 12 minutes). Transfer to a large bowl and beat until stiff. Gradually adding remaining 1/4 cup sugar, beat whipping cream in a large bowl until stiff. Fold egg white mixture into whipped cream mixture. Fold into chocolate mixture. Stir in marshmallows and almonds. Pour mousse into a serving bowl. Cover and chill until set.
Yield: 10 to 12 servings

A nutty vanilla wafer crust and a sweet custard filling are topped with fresh kiwi slices to make this colorful Kiwi Tart. A delicate apple jelly glaze is brushed over the fruit for a flavorful finishing touch.

KIWI TART

CRUST

- 2 cups finely crushed vanilla wafer cookies (about 48 cookies)
- 1/2 cup finely ground pecans
- 1/2 cup butter or margarine, melted

FILLING

- 1 cup milk
- 1 cup whipping cream
- 1 package (8 ounces) cream cheese, softened
- 1 vanilla bean, cut in half lengthwise
- 6 egg yolks
- 1 cup sugar
- 2 tablespoons all-purpose flour
- 6 kiwi fruit, peeled and cut into 1/8-inch slices

GLAZE

- 1 teaspoon cornstarch
- 1 teaspoon water
- 3 tablespoons apple jelly

For crust, preheat oven to 350 degrees. In a medium bowl, combine cookie crumbs, pecans, and butter. Press into bottom and up sides of an 11-inch tart pan with a removable bottom. Bake 12 to 15 minutes or until light brown. Cool completely on a wire rack. Remove crust from pan and place on a serving plate.

For filling, combine milk, whipping cream, cream cheese, and vanilla bean in a large saucepan. Stirring constantly, bring to a boil over medium heat; remove from heat. Cover and let stand 15 minutes.

Remove vanilla bean and use a sharp knife to scrape black seeds from bean into milk mixture. Return bean to milk mixture. In a small bowl, whisk egg yolks, sugar, and flour. Add about 1/2 cup milk mixture to egg mixture; stir until well blended. Add egg mixture to milk mixture in saucepan. Stirring constantly, bring to a boil over medium heat and cook 2 minutes or until thickened. Remove vanilla bean. Pour filling into crust. Cover and refrigerate until well chilled. Arrange kiwi fruit over filling.

For glaze, combine cornstarch and water in a small bowl; stir until smooth. In a small saucepan, melt jelly over medium heat. Whisk cornstarch mixture into jelly and cook until slightly thickened. Brush glaze evenly over kiwi fruit. Loosely cover and store in refrigerator.

Yield: 8 to 10 servings

CHOCOLATE-ORANGE CHEESECAKES

CHOCOLATE MINT LEAVES

- 1/4 cup semisweet chocolate chips
- 1 tablespoon butter or margarine
- 3 dozen fresh mint leaves, washed and patted dry

CHEESECAKES

- 6 large oranges (do not use navel oranges)
- 1 envelope unflavored gelatin
- 1/4 cup cold water
- 2 packages (8 ounces each) cream cheese, softened
- 2 cups sifted confectioners sugar
- 1/2 cup orange-flavored liqueur
- 1 teaspoon orange extract
- 1 package (6 ounces) semisweet chocolate chips, melted

TOPPING

- 1 package (3 ounces) cream cheese, softened
- 1 cup sifted confectioners sugar
- 1 teaspoon orange extract
- 1 cup whipping cream

For chocolate mint leaves, melt chocolate chips and butter in a small saucepan over low heat, stirring constantly. Use a small paintbrush to brush chocolate mixture onto tops of mint leaves. Transfer to waxed paper. Allow chocolate to harden in a cool, dry place.

For cheesecakes, cut oranges in half crosswise. Cut a thin slice off bottom of each orange half so orange half will sit flat. Leaving flesh and shells intact, use a small paring knife to remove flesh from orange halves; set aside.

In a small saucepan, sprinkle gelatin over water; allow to stand 1 minute. Stirring constantly, cook gelatin over low heat until gelatin dissolves. In a large bowl, beat cream cheese and confectioners sugar until fluffy. Add gelatin mixture, liqueur, and orange extract; beat until well blended. Gradually beat in melted chocolate chips. Spoon chocolate mixture into each orange shell. Cover and refrigerate until firm.

For topping, place a large bowl and beaters from an electric mixer in freezer until well chilled. In a medium bowl, beat cream cheese, confectioners sugar, and orange extract until fluffy. In chilled bowl, whip cream until stiff peaks form; beat in cream cheese mixture.

For each cheesecake, separate sections from 1 orange half; arrange on top of cheesecake. Spoon a heaping tablespoonful topping over each orange half. Garnish with chocolate leaves. Cover loosely with plastic wrap and refrigerate until ready to serve.

Yield: 12 servings

These Chocolate-Orange Cheesecakes are delightful! Orange flavoring enhances the chocolate cheesecake, which is served in orange shells topped with fresh fruit, whipped topping, and chocolate-coated mint leaves.

Banana Split Dessert is a delectable combination of bananas, ice cream, chocolate sauce, whipped cream, pecans, and maraschino cherries. Smooth, rich Almond Cappuccino is the perfect accompaniment to dessert. Cherry Cobbler Pie features a mouth-watering cream cheese filling and a delightful cinnamon crumb topping.

136

BANANA SPLIT DESSERT

CRUST
1½ cups graham cracker crumbs
2 tablespoons sugar
5 tablespoons butter or
    margarine, melted

FILLING
5 bananas, peeled and cut into
    ¼-inch slices
½ gallon cookies and cream ice
    cream, softened

FUDGE SAUCE
1 can (12 ounces) evaporated
    milk
1 package (6 ounces) semisweet
    chocolate chips
½ cup butter or margarine
2 cups sifted confectioners sugar

TOPPING
2 cups whipping cream
½ cup sugar
1 cup chopped pecans
1 jar (6 ounces) maraschino
    cherries, drained and
    chopped

For crust, combine cracker crumbs and sugar in a small bowl. Add melted butter; stir until crumbly. Press crumb mixture into bottom of a greased 9 x 13-inch baking dish.

For filling, arrange banana slices over crust. Spread ice cream over bananas. Cover and freeze until firm.

For fudge sauce, combine evaporated milk, chocolate chips, and butter in a medium saucepan. Stirring constantly, cook over low heat until smooth. Increase heat to medium. Gradually stir in confectioners sugar and bring to a boil. Stirring constantly, reduce heat to medium-low and boil 8 minutes. Remove from heat; cool to room temperature. Spread sauce over ice cream and return to freezer.

For topping, place a large bowl and beaters from an electric mixer in refrigerator until well chilled. In chilled bowl, beat whipping cream until soft peaks form. Gradually add sugar; beat until stiff peaks form. Spread whipped cream evenly over fudge sauce. Sprinkle pecans and cherries evenly over whipped cream. Cover and store in freezer until ready to serve.

To serve, remove from freezer 15 to 20 minutes before serving. Cut into about 2-inch squares.
Yield: about 24 servings

CHERRY COBBLER PIE

CRUST
2 cups graham cracker crumbs
½ cup all-purpose flour
½ cup butter or margarine, melted
¼ cup sugar

FILLING
1 package (8 ounces) cream
    cheese, softened
1½ cups sugar, divided
¼ cup cherry-flavored liqueur
1 tablespoon all-purpose flour
1 teaspoon dried lemon peel
2 cans (16 ounces each) tart red
    pitted cherries, undrained
¼ cup cornstarch

TOPPING
⅓ cup all-purpose flour
2 tablespoons sugar
2 tablespoons butter or
    margarine, melted
½ teaspoon vanilla extract
⅛ teaspoon ground cinnamon

For crust, combine cracker crumbs, flour, butter, and sugar in a medium bowl until well blended. Press into bottom and 2 inches up sides of a greased 10-inch springform pan; set aside.

For filling, beat cream cheese, ½ cup sugar, liqueur, flour, and lemon peel in a medium bowl until well blended. Spread cream cheese mixture over crust. Reserving ¼ cup juice, drain cherries. In a small bowl, combine cornstarch and reserved cherry juice; stir until smooth. In a medium saucepan, combine cherries and remaining 1 cup sugar. Stirring occasionally, cook over medium heat until sugar dissolves and mixture comes to a boil. Stirring constantly, add cornstarch mixture and cook until thickened. Pour over cream cheese mixture.

Preheat oven to 350 degrees. For topping, combine flour, sugar, butter, vanilla, and cinnamon in a small bowl. Sprinkle topping around edge of filling. Bake 30 minutes. Preheat broiler and broil 2 minutes or until topping is golden brown. Cool completely on a wire rack. Remove sides of pan and refrigerate until well chilled.
Yield: about 16 servings

ALMOND CAPPUCCINO

8 cups brewed coffee
4 cups evaporated skimmed milk
½ cup firmly packed brown sugar
1 tablespoon vanilla extract
1 teaspoon almond extract

In a large saucepan or Dutch oven, combine coffee, evaporated milk, and brown sugar. Stirring occasionally, cook over medium-high heat until mixture begins to boil; remove from heat. Stir in vanilla and almond extracts. Serve hot.
Yield: about 12 cups cappuccino

Your guests will find this beautifully decorated Chocolate-Mocha Cake irresistible! Loaded with chocolate chips, the devil's food cake is enhanced with coffee and coffee-flavored liqueur.

CHOCOLATE-MOCHA CAKE

CAKE
- 1 package (18.25 ounces) devil's food cake mix
- 3 eggs
- 1 cup coffee-flavored liqueur
- ½ cup vegetable oil
- ⅓ cup brewed coffee
- 1 cup semisweet chocolate chips

FROSTING
- 5¼ cups sifted confectioners sugar
- 1½ cups butter or margarine, softened
- 3 tablespoons milk

- 1 teaspoon vanilla extract
  Gold cord, garlands, ribbon, and jewel stones to decorate

Preheat oven to 350 degrees. For cake, combine cake mix, eggs, liqueur, oil, and coffee in a large bowl. Mix according to cake mix instructions. Stir in chocolate chips. Pour batter into a greased and floured 9 x 13-inch baking pan. Bake 35 to 40 minutes or until cake begins to pull away from sides of pan and top springs back when lightly

pressed. Cool in pan 10 minutes. Remove from pan and cool completely on a wire rack.

For frosting, combine confectioners sugar, butter, milk, and vanilla in a medium bowl; beat until smooth. Reserving 1 cup frosting, frost sides and top of cake. Spoon remaining frosting into a pastry bag fitted with a large star tip. Pipe decorative border along bottom edge of cake. Arrange decorations on top of cake. Remove decorations before serving.
Yield: about 16 servings

138

MEXICAN CHOCOLATE ANGEL FOOD CAKE

1³/₄ cups sifted confectioners sugar,
    divided
  1 cup sifted all-purpose flour
¹/₄ cup sifted cocoa
2¹/₄ teaspoons ground cinnamon,
    divided
1¹/₂ cups egg whites (10 to 12 large
    eggs)
1¹/₂ teaspoons cream of tartar
  1 teaspoon vanilla extract
  1 cup granulated sugar
    Sugared grapes to garnish

Preheat oven to 350 degrees. Sift
1¹/₂ cups confectioners sugar, flour,
cocoa, and 2 teaspoons cinnamon
3 times into a medium bowl.

In a large bowl, beat egg whites,
cream of tartar, and vanilla with an
electric mixer until soft peaks form.
Gradually add granulated sugar,
2 tablespoons at a time, and beat
until stiff peaks form.

Sift about ¹/₄ of confectioners sugar
mixture over egg white mixture; fold in
gently by hand. Continue to sift and
fold in confectioners sugar mixture in
small batches. Lightly spoon batter
into an ungreased 10-inch tube pan
and place on lower rack of oven.
Bake 40 to 45 minutes or until top
springs back when lightly touched.
Remove from oven and invert pan
onto neck of a bottle; cool completely.
Remove cake from pan, placing
bottom side up on a serving plate.

To decorate, combine remaining
¹/₄ cup confectioners sugar and
¹/₄ teaspoon cinnamon in a small
bowl. Place a 10-inch round paper
doily on top of cake and lightly sift
confectioners sugar mixture over
doily. Carefully remove doily. Garnish
with sugared grapes.
Yield: about 12 servings

Deliciously light in fat and calories, Mexican Chocolate Angel Food Cake is a divine completion for Christmas dinner. Its lacy decoration is created by sprinkling cinnamon and confectioners sugar over a paper doily.

There's only one word for this luscious frozen confection — Mmmm! A rich combination of flavors, Jamocha Toffee Mud Pie features a chocolate cookie crumb crust filled with coffee-flavored ice cream and chunks of chocolate-almond toffee. A chocolaty topping laced with coffee liqueur crowns this heavenly confection. You'll want to make an extra batch of the crunchy toffee for snacking, too. It's an unforgettable treat in its own right!

JAMOCHA TOFFEE MUD PIE

TOFFEE
- 1/2 cup plus 1 teaspoon butter or margarine, divided
- 1/2 cup sugar
- 1 tablespoon water
- 1/2 tablespoon light corn syrup
- 1/4 teaspoon almond extract
- 1/4 teaspoon vanilla extract
- 1 1/4 cups (about 10 ounces) sliced almonds, toasted
- 1/2 cup semisweet chocolate chips

CRUST
- 1 1/2 cups chocolate sandwich cookie crumbs (about 18 cookies)
- 3 tablespoons butter or margarine, melted

FILLING
- 1 quart coffee-flavored ice cream, softened

TOPPING
- 1 package (6 ounces) semisweet chocolate chips
- 1 can (5 ounces) evaporated milk
- 1/2 cup sugar
- 2 tablespoons coffee-flavored liqueur
- 1 tablespoon butter or margarine

For toffee, use 1 teaspoon butter to coat sides of a heavy large saucepan. Combine remaining 1/2 cup butter, sugar, water, and corn syrup in saucepan. Stirring constantly, cook over medium-low heat until sugar dissolves. Using a pastry brush dipped in hot water, wash down any sugar crystals on sides of pan. Attach a candy thermometer to pan, making sure thermometer does not touch bottom of pan. Increase heat to medium and bring to a boil. Cook, without stirring, until mixture reaches soft-crack stage (approximately 270 to 290 degrees). Test about 1/2 teaspoon mixture in ice water. Mixture will form hard threads in ice water but will soften when removed from the water. Remove from heat and stir in extracts and almonds. Pour onto a baking sheet lined with greased aluminum foil. Sprinkle chocolate chips over hot toffee. As chocolate melts, spread over toffee. Chill until

firm; break into small pieces.

Preheat oven to 350 degrees. For crust, combine cookie crumbs and melted butter in a small bowl. Press crumbs into bottom of a 9-inch springform pan. Bake 10 minutes. Place pan on a wire rack to cool completely.

For filling, reserve a few toffee pieces to garnish and combine remaining toffee pieces and ice cream in a large bowl. Wrap aluminum foil under and around outside of springform pan. Spoon ice cream mixture over crust. Cover with plastic wrap; freeze until firm.

For topping, combine chocolate chips, evaporated milk, and sugar in a heavy medium saucepan over medium heat. Stirring constantly, bring to a boil. Remove from heat; add liqueur and butter, stirring until butter melts. Remove pie from springform pan. Drizzle about 1/2 cup topping over pie. Garnish pie with reserved toffee pieces. Serve remaining topping warm with individual servings.

Yield: 10 to 12 servings

LEMON-FILLED PUMPKIN ROLL

CAKE

- 1 cup pasteurized egg substitute (equivalent to 4 eggs)
- 3/4 cup granulated sugar
- 2/3 cup canned pumpkin
- 1/4 cup nonfat buttermilk
- 2 tablespoons vegetable oil
- 3/4 cup all-purpose flour
- 2 1/2 teaspoons ground cinnamon
- 1 1/4 teaspoons baking powder
- 1/2 teaspoon salt
- 1/2 teaspoon ground nutmeg
- 1/4 teaspoon ground ginger
- 1 tablespoon confectioners sugar

FILLING

- 1 package (0.3 ounce) sugar-free lemon gelatin
- 1/2 cup boiling water
- 1 can (5 ounces) evaporated skimmed milk, chilled overnight
- 1 container (8 ounces) nonfat lemon yogurt
  Lemon slices to garnish

Preheat oven to 375 degrees. For cake, beat egg substitute in a large bowl at high speed of an electric mixer until foamy; gradually add granulated sugar. While mixing at low speed, add pumpkin, buttermilk, and oil. In a small bowl, combine flour, cinnamon, baking powder, salt, nutmeg, and ginger. Add flour mixture to egg mixture; beat until well blended. Spread batter evenly in a greased 10 1/2 x 15 1/2-inch jellyroll pan. Bake 12 to 15 minutes or until cake springs back when lightly touched. Sift confectioners sugar onto a smooth dish towel; immediately turn cake out onto towel. Beginning at 1 short edge, roll up warm cake in towel. Cool completely on a wire rack; wrap in plastic wrap and chill while preparing filling.

For filling, chill a small bowl and beaters from electric mixer in freezer. Add gelatin to boiling water in another small bowl; stir until gelatin dissolves. Cool gelatin mixture by placing bowl over ice. In chilled bowl from freezer, beat evaporated milk until stiff peaks form. Continue beating and quickly add gelatin mixture; fold in yogurt.

To assemble, carefully unroll cake, removing towel. Reserving about 1/2 cup filling to garnish, spread remaining lemon filling evenly over cake. Reroll cake. Spoon reserved filling into a pastry bag fitted with a small star tip. Garnish roll with lemon slices; pipe remaining filling onto lemon slices.

Yield: 8 to 10 servings

Lighten up your holiday menu with luscious Lemon-Filled Pumpkin Roll! The low-calorie treat features a fluffy filling wrapped in a spicy low-fat chiffon cake.

141

ORANGE-NUT POUND CAKE

CAKE

- 1 1/4 cups butter or margarine, softened
- 1 1/2 cups firmly packed brown sugar
- 6 eggs, separated
- 1 cup canned pumpkin
- 1/2 cup buttermilk
- 3 cups all-purpose flour
- 1 teaspoon ground cinnamon
- 1/2 teaspoon ground cardamom
- 1/2 teaspoon salt
- 1/2 teaspoon baking powder
- 1/2 teaspoon baking soda
- 1 cup finely chopped walnuts
- 1 tablespoon grated orange zest
- 1 tablespoon orange-flavored liqueur
- 1 teaspoon vanilla extract
- 1/2 cup granulated sugar

SYRUP

- 1/4 cup firmly packed brown sugar
- 1/4 cup butter or margarine
- 2 tablespoons water
- 1/4 cup orange-flavored liqueur

Preheat oven to 325 degrees. For cake, cream butter and brown sugar in a large bowl until fluffy. Reserving egg whites, add egg yolks, 1 at a time, beating well after each addition. Add pumpkin and buttermilk; stir until well blended. Sift flour, cinnamon, cardamom, salt, baking powder, and baking soda into a medium bowl. Add dry ingredients to creamed mixture; stir until well blended. Stir in walnuts, orange zest, liqueur, and vanilla; stir until well blended. Beat reserved egg whites until frothy; gradually add granulated sugar and beat until stiff peaks form. Fold beaten egg whites into cake batter. Pour batter into a greased and lightly floured 10-inch fluted tube pan. Bake 1 hour to 1 1/4 hours or until a toothpick inserted in center of cake comes out clean. Cool in pan 15 minutes; invert onto a serving plate.

For syrup, combine brown sugar, butter, and water in a small saucepan

Covered with a caramelized topping, custard-like Amaretto-Apricot Flan is a delicious alternative to traditional pumpkin or sweet potato pie. Moist Orange-Nut Pound Cake is saturated with an orange liqueur syrup.

over medium-high heat. Stirring frequently, bring mixture to a slow boil; boil about 2 minutes or until sugar dissolves. Remove from heat; stir in liqueur. While cake is still warm, use a wooden skewer to poke holes about 1 inch apart in cake; slowly spoon syrup over cake. Cool cake completely and cover. Allow cake to absorb syrup overnight.

Yield: about 16 servings

AMARETTO-APRICOT FLAN

- 3/4 cup plus 2 tablespoons sugar, divided
- 2 tablespoons water
- 1 can (17 ounces) apricot halves, drained
- 1 can (14 ounces) sweetened condensed milk
- 5 eggs
- 1/2 cup apricot nectar
- 5 tablespoons amaretto
- 1 tablespoon grated orange zest

¼ teaspoon salt
¼ teaspoon ground nutmeg
Canned apricot halves and
toasted slivered almonds to
garnish

Preheat oven to 150 degrees. Place a 9-inch round cake pan in oven to preheat. In a heavy medium skillet, combine ¾ cup sugar and water. Over medium-high heat, swirl skillet to dissolve sugar while allowing mixture to come to a rolling boil; do not stir. Using a pastry brush dipped in hot water, wash down any sugar crystals on sides of skillet. Continue to cook about 15 minutes or until syrup is a deep golden brown. Pour syrup into heated cake pan. Rotate pan to spread syrup evenly over bottom and halfway up sides; set aside.

Increase oven temperature to 350 degrees. Place apricots, condensed milk, eggs, apricot nectar, amaretto, orange zest, salt, nutmeg, and remaining 2 tablespoons sugar in a food processor. Pulse process until apricots are finely chopped; pour apricot mixture into pan over syrup. Place cake pan in a larger baking pan and fill baking pan with hot water to come halfway up sides of cake pan. Bake 1¼ to 1½ hours or until a knife inserted in center of flan comes out clean. Remove from oven; cool slightly. Cover and chill 8 hours or overnight.

To serve, place cake pan in a pan of very hot water about 5 minutes. Run a knife around edge of pan to loosen flan. Invert onto a serving plate. Garnish with apricots and toasted almonds.
Yield: 8 to 10 servings

COCONUT TORTE

1 sheet frozen puff pastry dough, thawed
4 eggs
1½ cups sugar
4½ cups frozen shredded unsweetened coconut, thawed
1 cup finely chopped almonds

Surrounded by a puff pastry crust, Coconut Torte has a delectable coconut-almond filling topped with peach preserves and whipped cream.

1 tablespoon butter, melted
1½ teaspoons vanilla extract
1 cup peach preserves
½ cup whipping cream, whipped

Preheat oven to 350 degrees. On a lightly floured surface, use a floured rolling pin to roll out pastry into a 12-inch-diameter circle. Place pastry in bottom and up sides of a greased 8-inch springform pan. Trim edges of pastry.

In a large bowl, beat eggs until foamy. Gradually add sugar, beating until fluffy. Stir in coconut, almonds, melted butter, and vanilla; pour into crust. Bake 55 to 60 minutes or until golden brown. Cool in pan 15 minutes. Remove sides of pan and cool completely. Spread peach preserves evenly over top of torte. Spoon whipped cream into a pastry bag fitted with a star tip; pipe whipped cream around top edge of torte. Refrigerate until ready to serve.
Yield: about 16 servings

Crowned with silk poinsettias and a golden bow, this Cranberry Cake is an impressive addition to a dessert buffet. Tangy cranberry sauce lends holiday flair to the flavorful spice cake.

144

CRANBERRY CAKE

CAKE

- 1/2 cup butter or margarine, softened
- 2 cups sugar
- 2 eggs
- 1 can (16 ounces) whole berry cranberry sauce
- 1 cup milk
- 2 1/2 cups all-purpose flour
- 1 1/2 teaspoons baking soda
- 1 1/2 teaspoons baking powder
- 1 teaspoon ground cinnamon
- 1/2 teaspoon ground allspice
- 1/4 teaspoon salt

FROSTING

- 3 cups butter or margarine, softened
- 5 tablespoons milk
- 2 tablespoons vanilla extract
- 12 cups sifted confectioners sugar

Preheat oven to 350 degrees. For cake, cream butter and sugar in a large bowl until fluffy using an electric mixer. Add eggs, 1 at a time, beating well after each addition. Beat in cranberry sauce and milk. Sift flour, baking soda, baking powder, cinnamon, allspice, and salt into a medium bowl. Add dry ingredients to creamed mixture, stirring until well blended. Pour batter into 3 greased and floured 9-inch round cake pans. Bake 35 to 40 minutes or until a toothpick inserted in center of cake comes out clean. Cool in pans 10 minutes. Remove from pans and cool completely on a wire rack.

For frosting, beat butter, milk, and vanilla in a large bowl using an electric mixer. Gradually add confectioners sugar; beat until smooth. Using about half of frosting, spread frosting between layers and on sides and top of cake.

To decorate cake with basket weave design, spoon remaining frosting into a pastry bag fitted with a basket weave tip. With serrated side of tip up, pipe a vertical stripe of frosting from top edge to bottom edge of cake. Pipe four 1-inch-long horizontal stripes over vertical stripe about 1 tip width apart **(Fig. 1)**.

Fig. 1

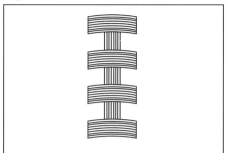

Overlapping ends of horizontal stripes, pipe another vertical stripe to the right of the first vertical stripe **(Fig. 2a)**. Pipe three 1-inch-long horizontal stripes as shown in **Fig. 2b.**

Fig. 2a   **Fig. 2b**

Repeat basket weave design until sides of cake are covered. Using a large star tip, pipe decorative border along bottom and top edges of cake.
Yield: about 20 servings

SPICY CHRISTMAS DRINK

- 2 cups water
- 1/2 cup sugar
- 3 cinnamon sticks
- 1 teaspoon whole cloves
- 1 gallon apple cider
- 1 can (12 ounces) frozen orange juice concentrate
- 1 can (12 ounces) frozen pineapple juice concentrate
- 1 can (6 ounces) frozen lemonade concentrate

Combine water and sugar in a stockpot. Stirring constantly, cook over medium-high heat 4 minutes or until sugar dissolves. Reduce heat to low. Add cinnamon sticks and cloves; cover and cook 15 minutes. Remove cinnamon and cloves. Stir in apple cider and orange, pineapple, and lemonade concentrates; heat until hot. Serve hot.
Yield: about 22 cups drink

Variation: Add 1 tablespoon apple brandy to each serving of prepared hot drink.

Cinnamon, cloves, and fruit juices make Spicy Christmas Drink a delicious winter warmer.

GIFTS OF GOOD TASTE

*N*othing says "Merry Christmas" like a homemade gift, and when that gift is from your kitchen, it's even better! We've provided a host of great ideas, including crispy cookies, sweet breads, seasoned vinegars, and much, much more. And for a creative presentation, simply pack the surprises in a decorated basket, a ready-made gift bag, or a pretty tin. Your friends, neighbors, and co-workers will look forward to these gifts of good taste!

Cut in a pencil shape and decorated with tinted icing, Hazelnut Cookies (recipe on page 148) make a cute gift for a teacher. Add winsome appeal to the present by packaging the treats in an apple-shaped basket with a slateboard tag.

HAZELNUT COOKIES

(Shown on pages 146 and 147)

COOKIES

- ³/₄ cup butter or margarine, softened
- ²/₃ cup sugar
- 1 egg
- 1 teaspoon vanilla extract
- ²/₃ cup finely ground hazelnuts
- 2¹/₄ cups all-purpose flour
- ¹/₄ teaspoon salt

ICING

- 4 cups confectioners sugar, sifted
- ¹/₂ cup plus 1 tablespoon milk
  Brown, pink, black, and yellow paste food coloring

Preheat oven to 350 degrees. For cookies, cream butter and sugar in a medium bowl until fluffy. Add egg and vanilla; beat until smooth. Stir in hazelnuts. Add flour and salt; stir until a soft dough forms. On a lightly floured surface, use a floured rolling pin to roll out dough to a 12-inch square. Cut out 1 x 6-inch cookies, cutting one end of each cookie into a point. Transfer to a greased baking sheet. Bake 12 to 15 minutes or until edges are lightly browned. Transfer cookies to a wire rack to cool.

For icing, combine confectioners sugar and milk in a medium bowl; stir until smooth. Transfer ¹/₄ cup icing to each of 3 small bowls; tint brown, pink, and black. Tint remaining icing yellow. Refer to photo and ice cookies, allowing icing to harden between each color. Store in an airtight container.

Yield: about 2 dozen cookies

PEACH-AMARETTO PRESERVES

- 3 pounds fresh peaches (about 10 peaches), peeled, pitted, and chopped (about 4 cups) **or** 2 packages (16 ounces each) frozen peaches, thawed and chopped

Made by combining almond flavorings with peaches and pecans, Peach-Amaretto Preserves are a yummy way to spread Christmas cheer. Deliver the preserves tucked in little silver baskets adorned with coordinating gift tags, ribbons, and other trims.

- 6 cups sugar
- 2 tablespoons freshly squeezed lemon juice
- 1¹/₂ cups chopped pecans
- ¹/₂ cup amaretto
- ¹/₂ teaspoon almond extract
- ¹/₈ teaspoon amaretto-flavored oil (used in candy making)

In a Dutch oven, combine peaches, sugar, and lemon juice. Stirring frequently, bring mixture to a boil; cook until sugar dissolves. Reduce heat to medium-low and simmer about 45 minutes or until peaches are translucent and syrup thickens. Continue to cook until syrup runs off the side of a metal spoon in a sheet. Remove from heat; skim off foam. Stir in pecans, amaretto, almond extract, and amaretto-flavored oil. Spoon preserves into heat-resistant jars; cover and cool to room temperature. Store in refrigerator.

Yield: about 4 pints preserves

PUMPKIN SEED BRITTLE

- ³/₄ cup purchased shelled pumpkin seeds
- 1¹/₂ cups sugar
- ¹/₂ cup light corn syrup
- ¹/₄ cup water
- 1¹/₂ tablespoons butter or margarine
- ¹/₂ teaspoon salt
- 1 teaspoon baking soda

Preheat oven to 350 degrees. To toast pumpkin seeds, spread pumpkin seeds on an ungreased baking sheet. Bake 5 to 8 minutes or until seeds are slightly darker in color. Cool completely on pan; set aside.

Butter sides of a heavy 3-quart saucepan. Combine sugar, corn syrup, and water in saucepan. Stirring constantly, cook over medium-low heat until sugar dissolves. Using a pastry brush dipped in hot water, wash down any sugar crystals on sides of pan. Attach a candy thermometer to pan, making sure thermometer does not touch bottom of pan. Increase heat to medium and bring to a boil. Cook, without stirring, until mixture reaches hard-crack stage (approximately 300 to 310 degrees) and turns light golden in color. Test about ¹/₂ teaspoon mixture in ice water. Mixture should form brittle threads in ice water and remain brittle when removed from the water. Remove from heat and stir in pumpkin seeds, butter, and salt; stir until butter melts. Stir in baking soda (mixture will foam). Pour candy into a buttered 10¹/₂ x 15¹/₂-inch jellyroll pan. Use a buttered spatula to spread candy to edges of pan. Cool completely. Break into pieces. Store in an airtight container.

Yield: about 1 pound brittle

Prepared with toasted pumpkin seeds, tasty Pumpkin Seed Brittle is great when you need lots of little gifts to pass out at work or school. Package the goodies in ribbon-tied gift bags and distribute them from a decorated basket.

A gift to be savored, Herb Bread is a rich wheat bread with rosemary and thyme flavorings and a fresh sage garnish. It's extra good accompanied by our creamy Herb Butter.

HERB BREAD

Fresh sage leaves to decorate
2 packages dry yeast
1/3 cup warm water
5 cups bread flour
1 cup whole-wheat flour
2 tablespoons dried rosemary leaves, crushed
1 tablespoon dried thyme leaves, crushed
2 1/2 teaspoons salt
1 1/2 cups warm milk
1/2 cup honey
1/4 cup vegetable oil
Vegetable cooking spray
1 egg, beaten

Press fresh sage leaves between paper towels 8 hours or overnight.

In a small bowl, dissolve yeast in 1/3 cup warm water. In a large bowl, combine bread flour, whole-wheat flour, rosemary, thyme, and salt. Add yeast mixture, milk, honey, and oil to dry ingredients. Stir until a soft dough forms. Turn onto a lightly floured surface and knead 5 minutes or until dough becomes smooth and elastic. Place in a large bowl sprayed with cooking spray, turning once to coat top of dough. Cover and let rise in a warm place (80 to 85 degrees) 1 hour or until doubled in size.

Turn dough onto a lightly floured surface and punch down. Divide dough into thirds. Shape each piece of dough into a loaf and place in a greased 5 x 9-inch loaf pan. Spray tops of loaves with cooking spray, cover, and let rise in a warm place 1 hour or until doubled in size.

Preheat oven to 350 degrees. Brush tops of loaves with egg. Arrange pressed sage on tops of loaves; brush sage with egg. Bake 25 to 30 minutes or until bread sounds hollow when tapped. Serve warm or transfer to a wire rack to cool completely. Store in an airtight container. Give with Herb Butter.
Yield: 3 loaves bread

HERB BUTTER

1 tablespoon plus 2 teaspoons
   dried rosemary leaves,
   crushed
1 tablespoon dried thyme leaves,
   crushed
1½ teaspoons ground cardamom
1½ cups butter, softened
½ cup whipping cream

Process rosemary, thyme, and
cardamom in a food processor until
finely ground. In a medium bowl, use
an electric mixer to cream butter until
fluffy. With electric mixer running,
gradually add whipping cream; beat
until fluffy. Stir in herb mixture. Spoon
into jars or small ramekins. Cover
and chill. Give with Herb Bread.
Yield: about 2½ cups herb butter

PUDDING CANDY

3 cups sugar
1¼ cups half and half
2 tablespoons light corn syrup
2 tablespoons butter or
   margarine, divided
½ cup raisins
½ cup chopped pecans
½ cup flaked coconut
½ cup chopped red and green
   candied cherries

Butter sides of a heavy medium
saucepan. Combine sugar, half and
half, corn syrup, and 1 tablespoon
butter in saucepan. Stirring constantly,
cook over medium-low heat until
sugar dissolves. Using a pastry brush
dipped in hot water, wash down any
sugar crystals on sides of pan. Attach
a candy thermometer to pan, making
sure thermometer does not touch
bottom of pan. Increase heat to
medium and bring to a boil. Cook,
without stirring, until mixture reaches
soft-ball stage (approximately
234 to 240 degrees). Test about
½ teaspoon mixture in ice water.
Mixture will easily form a ball in ice
water but flatten when held in your
hand. Remove from heat and add

A present that's sure to sweeten the season, delectable Pudding Candy is packed with raisins, pecans, and coconut. Red and green candied cherries add Christmas flair.

remaining 1 tablespoon butter; do not
stir until mixture cools to approximately
200 degrees. Using medium speed
of an electric mixer, beat candy until
thickened. Stir in raisins, pecans,
coconut, and cherries. Pour into a
buttered 7 x 11-inch baking pan.
Cool completely. Cut into 1-inch
squares. Store in an airtight container
in refrigerator.
Yield: about 5 dozen pieces candy

Spiced with ginger, this Cherry-Nut Cheese Ball Mix makes a sweet dessert spread when blended with cream cheese. To share this unique holiday treat, give a ready-to-eat cheese ball to enjoy now and include a bag of mix and instructions for preparing another one later.

CHERRY-NUT CHEESE BALL MIX

1¼ cups dried cherries (available at gourmet food stores)
1¼ cups finely chopped walnuts
2 teaspoons ground ginger, divided
  Vanilla wafers to serve

In a medium bowl, combine cherries and walnuts. Divide mixture evenly into 2 small airtight containers.

Stir 1 teaspoon ginger into each container and seal. Give with serving instructions.

Yield: about 2½ cups mix, enough to make 2 cheese balls

To serve: For each cheese ball, combine 1¼ cups mix with one 8-ounce package softened cream cheese. Shape into a ball; wrap in plastic wrap and refrigerate until firm. To serve, let stand at room temperature 20 to 30 minutes or until softened. Serve with vanilla wafers.

Yield: 1 cheese ball

A batch of Green Chile-Corn Dip will rustle up lots of Southwestern flavor for a friend. Teamed with tortilla chips, the mildly spiced dip can be presented in a Western-style gift basket with red bandanna napkins and napkin rings gussied up with conchas, raffia bows, and chile peppers.

GREEN CHILE-CORN DIP

$^1/_2$ cup plus 2 tablespoons drained canned whole kernel corn, divided

1 cup nonfat cottage cheese

2 tablespoons picante sauce

$^1/_4$ teaspoon garlic powder

$^1/_8$ teaspoon ground cumin

1 can (4$^1/_2$ ounces) chopped green chiles

4 tablespoons diced sweet red pepper, divided

Tortilla chips to serve

Process $^1/_2$ cup corn, cottage cheese, picante sauce, garlic powder, and cumin in a food processor until puréed. Transfer to a medium bowl. Stir in chiles, 2 tablespoons red pepper, and remaining 2 tablespoons corn. Garnish with remaining 2 tablespoons red pepper. Cover and chill. Serve chilled with chips.

Yield: about 2$^1/_3$ cups dip

Flavored with garlic, Parmesan cheese, or toasted almonds, these savory Cheese Spreads make delightful gifts. Each is made by adding ingredients to one basic spread. Miniature flowerpots make cute gift containers!

CHEESE SPREADS

BASIC SPREAD
- 2 packages (8 ounces each) cream cheese, softened
- 1/2 cup sour cream
- 3 tablespoons mayonnaise

Beat cream cheese, sour cream, and mayonnaise in a medium bowl until smooth. Use Basic Spread to make each of the following recipes.
Yield: about 2²/₃ cups spread

GARLIC
- 1 cup Basic Spread
- 1¹/₂ teaspoons garlic salt
- 1 teaspoon fines herbes
- 1/8 teaspoon hot pepper sauce
  Fines herbes to garnish

Combine basic spread, garlic salt, 1 teaspoon fines herbes, and pepper sauce in a small bowl; stir until well blended. Transfer to a serving container; sprinkle with fines herbes to garnish. Serve with assorted crackers.

CHEESE
- 1 cup Basic Spread
- 1/3 cup grated Parmesan cheese
- 1 teaspoon Worcestershire sauce
- 3/4 teaspoon onion salt
  Grated Parmesan cheese to garnish

Combine basic spread, 1/3 cup Parmesan cheese, Worcestershire sauce, and onion salt; stir until well blended. Transfer to a serving container; sprinkle with Parmesan cheese to garnish. Serve with assorted crackers or wedges of red apple.

ALMOND
- 2/3 cup Basic Spread
- 1/4 cup butter, softened
- 1/4 cup sugar
- 1/8 cup golden raisins
- 1/8 cup slivered almonds
  Raisins or almonds to garnish

Combine basic spread, butter, sugar, 1/8 cup raisins, and 1/8 cup almonds; stir until well blended. Transfer to a serving container; sprinkle with raisins or almonds to garnish. Serve with assorted fruits or crackers.

IRISH SMOOTHIE

- 2 cups whipping cream
- 1 cup sweetened condensed milk
- 3/4 cup Irish whiskey
- 1/2 cup brandy
- 2 tablespoons chocolate syrup
- 1 tablespoon instant coffee granules
- 1 teaspoon vanilla extract
- 1 teaspoon almond extract

Combine whipping cream, condensed milk, whiskey, brandy, chocolate syrup, coffee granules, and extracts in a blender until well mixed. Pour into a gift container. Cover and store in refrigerator.

Yield: about 4 1/4 cups liqueur

CHOCOLATE CUPS

Chocolate cups also make perfect containers for chocolate mousse or fresh fruit.

- 4 ounces semisweet baking chocolate
- 1 tablespoon butter
- 8 foil muffin cups
  Ice cream, Irish Smoothie, and fresh sweet cherries to serve

In a heavy small saucepan, melt chocolate and butter over low heat, stirring constantly (do not overheat). Cool until slightly thickened. Place 1 tablespoon chocolate mixture in a foil cup; spread over bottom and sides. Place another foil cup on top of chocolate and press lightly. Repeat with remaining chocolate mixture. Refrigerate or freeze until firm.

To serve, carefully remove foil liners. Fill each chocolate cup with ice cream; top with Irish Smoothie and a cherry.

Yield: 4 chocolate cups

This rich, creamy Irish Smoothie is delicious stirred into coffee or poured over ice cream. Include some Chocolate Cups for serving ice cream and present the beverage in an old-fashioned milk bottle for a tasty surprise.

A bottle of homemade Raspberry Liqueur is a tasteful gift. For an extra-special treat, include a bag of delicate Cream Puffs to serve with ice cream and fruity Raspberry Liqueur Sauce. A pair of liqueur glasses makes an elegant finish.

RASPBERRY LIQUEUR

Raspberry Liqueur is delicious served over vanilla or chocolate ice cream. We filled our Cream Puffs with creamy vanilla ice cream and topped them with Raspberry Liqueur Sauce.

2   packages (10 ounces each) frozen red raspberries in syrup, thawed
1 1/2   cups sugar
1/2   lemon, sliced
1 1/2   cups vodka

Drain raspberry juice into a large microwave-safe bowl; reserve raspberries. Add sugar and lemon slices to raspberry juice. Stirring often, microwave on high power (100%) 3 to 5 minutes or until sugar dissolves and mixture boils. Skim any foam from top of mixture and remove lemon slices. Add reserved raspberries and vodka to juice mixture; pour into gift bottle. Shaking bottle each week, cover and store in refrigerator 1 month before serving. Before serving, pour contents through a fine strainer. Store in refrigerator. Give with recipe for Cream Puffs With Raspberry Liqueur Sauce.
Yield: about 3 cups liqueur

CREAM PUFFS WITH RASPBERRY LIQUEUR SAUCE

Cream Puff Pastry is easy to make. Bake several batches and store in the freezer for gift-giving or for holiday entertaining.

RASPBERRY LIQUEUR SAUCE
1   package (10 ounces) frozen red raspberries in syrup, thawed
4   tablespoons currant jelly
3   tablespoons Raspberry Liqueur
1/2   teaspoon freshly squeezed lemon juice
1   tablespoon cornstarch
1   tablespoon water

CREAM PUFF PASTRY
1   cup water
6   tablespoons butter
1/8   teaspoon salt
1/8   teaspoon sugar
1   cup all-purpose flour
4   eggs
Ice cream to serve

For raspberry liqueur sauce, heat raspberries in a small saucepan. Stir in jelly, liqueur, and lemon juice; bring to a boil. Dissolve cornstarch in water in a small bowl; add to raspberry mixture. Cook until thickened, stirring constantly. Transfer to a medium bowl; cover and set aside.

Preheat oven to 350 degrees. For cream puff pastry, bring water, butter, salt, and sugar to a boil in a medium saucepan; immediately remove from heat. Stir in flour all at once. Stirring constantly, return pan to heat 30 seconds. Remove from heat. Beat in eggs, 1 at a time, until mixture is a smooth paste. Use a metal spoon to drop heaping tablespoons of mixture onto greased nonstick baking sheets. Bake 45 minutes. Remove puffs from baking sheets and cool on wire racks. Serve puffs with ice cream and raspberry liqueur sauce. Store in an airtight container or freeze.
Yield: about 24 two-inch puffs and about 1 1/2 cups sauce

HEARTWARMING TEA MIX

1   jar (15 ounces) orange-flavored powdered instant breakfast drink
1   cup sugar
1   cup unsweetened powdered instant tea
1/2   cup presweetened lemonade-flavored soft drink mix
1   teaspoon pineapple extract
1   teaspoon coconut extract

Process orange drink, sugar, tea, lemonade mix, and extracts in a food processor until well blended. Give with serving instructions.
Yield: about 4 1/4 cups tea mix
To serve: Pour 6 ounces hot water over 1 rounded tablespoon tea mix; stir until well blended.

Heartwarming Tea Mix gets its refreshing appeal from a blend of orange, lemon, pineapple, and coconut flavors. To complete the gift, package the mix with a mug reflecting the peace and harmony of the season.

HERBED LEMON VINEGAR

We made our beautiful lemon vinegar with fresh tarragon leaves.

- 4 cups white wine vinegar
- 4 lemons
- 4 small sprigs fresh dill weed, basil, or tarragon leaves

In a medium saucepan, heat vinegar to boiling. Use a small knife to peel each lemon in a continuous spiral. Place lemon peel and herb sprigs in heat-resistant gift bottle. Pour vinegar mixture into bottle. Cover and chill at least 2 days to allow flavors to blend. Store in refrigerator. Give with recipe for Walnut Citrus Salad.
Yield: about 4 cups vinegar

WALNUT CITRUS SALAD

Tangy orange and grapefruit sections are combined with fresh, crisp salad greens.

LEMON DRESSING
- 3/4 cup vegetable oil
- 1/4 cup olive oil
- 1/4 cup Herbed Lemon Vinegar
- 1/2 cup honey
  Juice of 1 lemon

SALAD
- 1 cup walnut halves
- 1/4 cup butter
- 6 cups mixed salad greens pieces (we used romaine, bibb, and iceberg)
- 1 medium red onion, thinly sliced
- 1 cup fresh orange sections
- 1 cup fresh grapefruit sections

These versatile vinegars will spark the imaginations of the cooks on your list! For a zesty holiday treat, give a bottle of Herbed Lemon, Blueberry, or Garlic Vinegar along with our recipes for complementary dishes — Walnut Citrus Salad, Fresh Fruit with Blueberry Dressing, and Quick Turkey Salad (not shown).

For lemon dressing, whisk oils, herbed lemon vinegar, honey, and lemon juice in a small bowl until well blended. Store in an airtight container.

For salad, sauté walnuts in butter in a small skillet until walnuts are lightly toasted. Place salad greens in a large bowl; add onion. Toss mixture with lemon dressing until coated. Add walnuts and fruit; toss again.
Yield: about 1 3/4 cups lemon dressing and about 6 servings salad

BLUEBERRY VINEGAR

Rice wine vinegar is best to use when making a fruit-flavored vinegar. Vinegar should have at least a 5 percent acidity level.

- 2 cups frozen blueberries, thawed and divided
- 4 cups rice or white wine vinegar

In a large saucepan, combine 1 cup blueberries with vinegar. Heat 10 minutes, but do not boil. Place remaining 1 cup blueberries in a heat-resistant gift bottle. Strain vinegar mixture through a fine strainer; pour into bottle. Cover and store in refrigerator. Give with recipe for Fresh Fruit with Blueberry Dressing.
Yield: about 4 cups vinegar

FRESH FRUIT WITH BLUEBERRY DRESSING

- 1/2 cup mayonnaise
- 1/2 cup whipping cream
- 2 tablespoons Blueberry Vinegar
- 2 teaspoons confectioners sugar
  Fresh apples, kiwi, and grapes to serve

In a small bowl, whisk mayonnaise, whipping cream, blueberry vinegar, and confectioners sugar until well blended. Pour over sliced fresh fruit.
Yield: about 1 cup dressing

GARLIC VINEGAR

- 4 cloves garlic, trimmed to fit in gift bottle
  Wooden skewer to fit in gift bottle
- 4 cups red wine vinegar

Place garlic on skewer; carefully insert into a heat-resistant gift bottle. In a large saucepan, bring vinegar to a boil. Pour vinegar into bottle. Cover and store in refrigerator. Give with recipe for Quick Turkey Salad.
Yield: about 4 cups vinegar

QUICK TURKEY SALAD

GARLIC DRESSING
- 2 teaspoons sugar
- 1 clove garlic, minced
- 1/2 teaspoon dry mustard
- 4 tablespoons Garlic Vinegar
- 1/2 teaspoon Worcestershire sauce
  Salt and ground black pepper
- 1/2 cup vegetable oil

SALAD
- 3 cups cooked chopped turkey
- 1/2 pound red seedless grapes, sliced
- 1/2 cup stuffed green olives, sliced
- 1/2 cup sliced almonds, toasted
- 3 green onions, chopped, including tops

For garlic dressing, combine sugar and garlic into a paste in a small bowl. Add dry mustard, garlic vinegar, and Worcestershire sauce. Salt and pepper to taste; whisk in oil.

For salad, combine turkey, grapes, olives, almonds, and green onions in a serving bowl. Add dressing and toss. Refrigerate at least 1 hour before serving.
Yield: about 3/4 cup dressing and 4 to 6 servings salad

Guaranteed to please even the most discriminating palates, a bottle of homemade Amaretto makes an impressive gift. Include a rich, creamy Double Chocolate Cheesecake flavored with the amaretto, and your surprise will be especially memorable.

AMARETTO

This smooth liqueur is delicious alone, in coffee, or served over ice cream.

- 2 cups sugar
- 1 cup water
- 3/4 ounce amaretto extract (available at winemaking supply stores)
- 2 cups vodka

In a medium saucepan, combine sugar and water. Bring to a boil over medium heat and stir 3 to 4 minutes. Remove from heat. Stir in amaretto extract and vodka. Pour into a gift bottle. Cover and store in refrigerator 1 month before serving. Store in refrigerator after opening.

Yield: about 4 cups liqueur

DOUBLE CHOCOLATE CHEESECAKE

You can bake this treat for gifts in six 4 1/2-inch-diameter tart pans or in one 9-inch springform pan.

OATMEAL CRUST
- 1 cup quick-cooking oats
- 1/3 cup chopped almonds
- 1/3 cup firmly packed light brown sugar
- 4 tablespoons butter, softened
- 1/2 teaspoon ground cinnamon

CHOCOLATE CHEESE FILLING
- 2 packages (8 ounces each) cream cheese
- 1/2 cup sugar
- 1/4 cup Amaretto
- 4 eggs
- 4 ounces semisweet baking chocolate, melted

CHOCOLATE GLAZE
- 4 ounces sweet dark baking chocolate, broken into pieces
- 1 tablespoon butter
- 3 tablespoons whipping cream
- 1/4 teaspoon Amaretto

Preheat oven to 350 degrees. For oatmeal crust, process oats, almonds, brown sugar, butter, and cinnamon in a food processor until well blended. Press mixture into bottoms of six 4 1/2-inch-diameter tart pans or one 9-inch springform pan (mixture should be crumbly, but will hold together when pressed into pan). Bake 6 to 8 minutes. Cool on a wire rack.

Preheat oven to 350 degrees. For chocolate cheese filling, beat cream cheese, sugar, and Amaretto in a large bowl until well blended. Add eggs, 1 at a time, beating well after each addition. Add melted chocolate; stir until mixture is thick and smooth. Spoon into baked crust. Bake 30 to 35 minutes or until center is firm. Cool on a wire rack.

For chocolate glaze, melt chocolate and butter in a heavy small saucepan over low heat; stir until smooth. Remove pan from heat; stir in whipping cream and Amaretto. Spread glaze over cooled cheesecake. Chill several hours before serving.

Yield: six 4 1/2-inch cheesecakes

CAPPUCCINO COFFEE MIX

- 1/2 cup instant coffee granules
- 1/2 teaspoon dried orange peel
- 1 cup non-dairy powdered creamer
- 3/4 cup sugar
- 1/2 teaspoon ground cinnamon

Process coffee and orange peel in a food processor until finely ground. Add creamer, sugar, and cinnamon; process until well blended. Store in an airtight container. Give with serving instructions.

Yield: about 1 2/3 cups coffee mix

To serve: Pour 6 ounces hot water over 2 heaping teaspoons coffee mix; stir until well blended.

A coffee lover is sure to enjoy the delightful beverage made from our instant Cappuccino Coffee Mix, which combines orange and cinnamon flavors. Slip a bag of the mix into a decorative basket along with a festive mug.

161

162

MEXICAN BEAN SOUP MIX

BEAN SOUP MIX
- 1 pound black beans
- 1 pound red beans
- 1 pound great Northern beans

SEASONING MIX
- 3 tablespoons dried parsley flakes, divided
- 4 1/2 teaspoons chili powder, divided
- 3 teaspoons salt, divided
- 1 1/2 teaspoons crushed dried red pepper flakes, divided
- 3/4 teaspoon garlic powder, divided
- 3/4 teaspoon ground black pepper, divided

For bean soup mix, combine all ingredients in a large bowl. Place about 2 heaping cups beans in each of 3 resealable plastic bags.

For seasoning mix, combine 1 tablespoon parsley, 1 1/2 teaspoons chili powder, 1 teaspoon salt, 1/2 teaspoon red pepper flakes, 1/4 teaspoon garlic powder, and 1/4 teaspoon black pepper in each of 3 small resealable plastic bags.

Give 1 bag of beans with 1 bag of seasoning mix and recipe for Mexican Bean Soup.
Yield: about 6 cups bean soup mix and about 6 1/2 tablespoons seasoning mix

MEXICAN BEAN SOUP

- 1 bag (about 2 cups) Mexican Bean Soup Mix
- 1 pound bulk pork sausage
- 2 onions, quartered
- 2 cloves garlic, minced

This spicy Southwestern "dinner in a basket" includes Mexican Bean Soup Mix, Mexican Corn Bread Mix, and a bag of melt-in-your-mouth Pralines. Include a set of colorful, inexpensive tableware for a quick holiday meal.

- 1 can (16 ounces) whole peeled tomatoes
- 1 can (4 1/2 ounces) chopped green chiles
- 1 bag (about 2 tablespoons) Seasoning Mix
  Salt and ground black pepper to taste

Rinse bean soup mix. Place beans in a Dutch oven and cover with water; soak overnight.

In a large skillet, brown sausage, onions, and garlic. Drain beans and return to Dutch oven. Add sausage mixture, tomatoes, green chiles, and seasoning mix to beans. Add enough water to cover. Stirring occasionally, simmer 3 to 4 hours or until beans are tender. Add more water as needed. Salt and pepper to taste.
Yield: 8 to 10 servings

PRALINES

- 1 3/4 cups granulated sugar
- 1 1/4 cups firmly packed brown sugar
- 1 cup evaporated milk
- 1/2 cup butter or margarine
- 2 tablespoons dark corn syrup
- 4 cups pecan halves

In a heavy large saucepan, combine granulated sugar, brown sugar, evaporated milk, butter, and corn syrup. Stirring occasionally, bring to a boil over medium heat. Attach a candy thermometer to pan, making sure thermometer does not touch bottom of pan. Cook, without stirring, until mixture reaches soft-ball stage (approximately 234 to 240 degrees). Test about 1/2 teaspoon of mixture in ice water. Mixture will easily form a ball in ice water but will flatten when held in your hand. Transfer to a heat-resistant medium bowl and beat with an electric mixer about 5 minutes. Stir in pecans. Drop by teaspoonfuls onto waxed paper; cool completely. Store in an airtight container.
Yield: about 48 small pralines

MEXICAN CORN BREAD MIX

- 2 cups yellow cornmeal
- 1/2 cup all-purpose flour
- 1 tablespoon sugar
- 2 teaspoons baking powder
- 1 teaspoon salt
- 1 teaspoon ground red pepper
- 1/2 teaspoon baking soda

In a large bowl, combine cornmeal, flour, sugar, baking powder, salt, red pepper, and baking soda. Place in a resealable plastic bag. Give mix with recipe for Mexican Corn Bread.
Yield: about 2 1/2 cups mix

MEXICAN CORN BREAD

- 2 tablespoons butter or margarine
- 1 bag (about 2 1/2 cups) Mexican Corn Bread Mix
- 1 can (12 ounces) beer
- 2 eggs, lightly beaten

Preheat oven to 425 degrees. Place butter in an 8-inch round baking pan or skillet. Place pan in oven to melt butter and to heat pan. In a medium bowl, combine corn bread mix, beer, and eggs. Stir just until blended. Pour into hot pan. Bake 25 to 30 minutes or until lightly browned. Serve warm.
Yield: 6 to 8 servings

"STAINED GLASS" BRITTLE

- ³/₄ cup coarsely crushed assorted fruit-flavored, ring-shaped hard candies (about 7 rolls)
- 1½ cups sugar
- ½ cup light corn syrup
- ¼ cup water
- 1½ tablespoons butter or margarine
- ½ teaspoon salt
- 1 teaspoon baking soda

Spread crushed candies evenly in a buttered 10½ x 15½-inch jellyroll pan. Butter sides of a 3-quart heavy saucepan or Dutch oven. Combine sugar, corn syrup, and water in pan. Stirring constantly, cook over medium-low heat until sugar dissolves. Using a pastry brush dipped in hot water, wash down any sugar crystals on sides of pan. Attach a candy thermometer to pan, making sure thermometer does not touch bottom of pan. Increase heat to medium and bring to a boil. Cook, without stirring, until mixture reaches hard-crack stage (approximately 300 to 310 degrees) and turns light golden in color. Test about ½ teaspoon mixture in ice water. Mixture should form brittle threads in ice water and will remain brittle when removed from the water. Remove from heat and add butter and salt; stir until butter melts. Add baking soda (mixture will foam); stir until baking soda dissolves. Pour hot mixture over candies. Using a buttered spatula, spread candy to edges of pan. Cool completely. Break into pieces. Store in an airtight container.

Yield: about 1¼ pounds brittle

Crushed hard candies add bright colors and fruity flavors to "Stained Glass" Brittle, a variation of a traditional favorite that's perfect for sharing.

164

Moist coconut-flavored Snowball Cupcakes get their wintry appeal from fluffy frosting and a blizzard of shredded coconut.

SNOWBALL CUPCAKES

1 package (18.25 ounces) yellow cake mix
3 eggs
1/3 cup vegetable oil
1 can (8 1/2 ounces) cream of coconut
1 cup sour cream
1 package (7.2 ounces) fluffy white frosting mix
1 3/4 cups flaked coconut
Candied cherry halves to decorate

Preheat oven to 350 degrees. Combine cake mix, eggs, and oil in a large bowl; beat until well blended. Add cream of coconut and sour cream; beat until smooth. Line muffin pan with aluminum foil muffin cups; fill cups half full. Bake 16 to 18 minutes or until a toothpick inserted in center of cupcake comes out clean. Cool in pan on a wire rack.

In a medium bowl, prepare frosting according to package directions. Dip tops of cupcakes into icing, then into coconut. Decorate with candied cherry halves. Store in a single layer in an airtight container.
Yield: about 3 dozen cupcakes

Swirls of rich chocolate and vanilla make Marble Fudge an extra-special offering.

MARBLE FUDGE

2 cups sugar
1 cup whipping cream
1/2 cup butter or margarine
1 tablespoon light corn syrup
1 teaspoon vanilla extract
1/2 cup semisweet chocolate chips, melted

Butter sides of a large stockpot. Combine sugar, whipping cream, butter, and corn syrup in pan. Stirring constantly, cook over medium-low heat until sugar dissolves. Using a pastry brush dipped in hot water, wash down any sugar crystals on sides of pan. Attach a candy thermometer to pan, making sure thermometer does not touch bottom of pan. Increase heat to medium and bring to a boil. Cook, without stirring, until mixture reaches soft-ball stage (approximately 234 to 240 degrees). Test about 1/2 teaspoon mixture in ice water. Mixture will easily form a ball in ice water but flatten when held in your hand. Place pan in 2 inches of cold water in sink. Add vanilla; do not stir. Cool to approximately 110 degrees. Remove from sink. Using medium speed of an electric mixer, beat until fudge thickens and begins to lose its gloss. Pour into a buttered 8-inch square baking pan. Drizzle melted chocolate over fudge. Using tip of a knife, gently swirl chocolate into fudge. Chill until firm. Cut into 1-inch squares. Store in an airtight container in refrigerator.

Yield: about 5 dozen pieces fudge

A loaf of Whole Grain Bread is a mouth-watering gift from your hearth. You'll also want to include a batch of the mix and the recipe so your friends can prepare more.

WHOLE GRAIN BREAD MIX

1 1/2 cups all-purpose flour
1/2 cup whole-wheat flour
1/4 cup old-fashioned oats
2 tablespoons yellow cornmeal
2 tablespoons wheat germ
2 tablespoons unprocessed bran
2 tablespoons firmly packed
    brown sugar
1 teaspoon salt
1 package quick-rise dry yeast

Combine flours, oats, cornmeal, wheat germ, bran, brown sugar, salt, and yeast in a large bowl; stir until well blended. Store in an airtight container in a cool place. Give with baking instructions.

Yield: about 2 1/2 cups bread mix, makes 1 loaf bread

To bake bread: Place bread mix in a large bowl. In a small saucepan, heat 1 cup milk and 2 tablespoons vegetable oil until very warm (120 to 130 degrees). Add milk mixture to bread mix; stir until a soft dough forms. Turn onto a lightly floured surface and knead 5 minutes or until dough becomes smooth and elastic. Cover and allow dough to rest 10 minutes. Shape dough into a loaf

and place in a greased 4 1/2 x 8 1/2-inch loaf pan. Spray top of dough with cooking spray, cover, and let rise in a warm place (80 to 85 degrees) 50 minutes or until doubled in size.

Preheat oven to 375 degrees. Brush top of loaf with a beaten egg. Bake 25 to 30 minutes or until bread is golden brown and sounds hollow when tapped. Serve warm or transfer to a wire rack to cool completely. Store in an airtight container.

CARAMEL-CHOCOLATE LAYERED FUDGE

CARAMEL FUDGE
    2 cups sugar
  1/2 cup evaporated milk
    5 tablespoons light corn syrup
    3 tablespoons butter or margarine
    1 tablespoon honey
  1/4 teaspoon salt
    1 teaspoon vanilla extract
    1 cup finely chopped walnuts

CHOCOLATE FUDGE
    4 cups sugar
    1 cup evaporated milk
  1/3 cup light corn syrup
    6 tablespoons butter or margarine
    2 tablespoons honey
  1/2 teaspoon salt
    1 teaspoon vanilla extract
 1 1/2 cups semisweet chocolate chips
    1 cup finely chopped walnuts

For caramel fudge, butter sides of a large stockpot. Combine sugar, evaporated milk, corn syrup, butter, honey, and salt in pan. Stirring constantly, cook over medium-low heat until sugar dissolves. Using a pastry brush dipped in hot water, wash down any sugar crystals on sides of pan. Attach a candy thermometer to pan, making sure thermometer does not touch bottom of pan. Increase heat to medium and bring to a boil. Cook, without stirring, until mixture reaches soft-ball stage (approximately 234 to 240 degrees). Test about 1/2 teaspoon mixture in ice water. Mixture will easily form a ball in ice water but flatten when held in your hand. Place pan in 2 inches of cold water in sink. Add vanilla; do not stir. Cool to approximately 110 degrees. Using medium speed of an electric mixer, beat until fudge thickens and begins to lose its gloss. Pour into a buttered 8 x 11-inch baking dish. Sprinkle walnuts evenly over top.

This rich Caramel-Chocolate Layered Fudge is two treats in one!

For chocolate fudge, follow instructions for caramel fudge until mixture cools to approximately 110 degrees. Add chocolate chips and beat using medium speed of an electric mixer until fudge thickens and begins to lose its gloss. Pour chocolate fudge over caramel fudge. Sprinkle walnuts evenly over top. Allow to harden. Cut into 1-inch squares. Store in an airtight container in refrigerator.

Yield: about 7 dozen pieces fudge

It only takes a few minutes to make a batch of microwave Candied Christmas Popcorn, and it's sure to be a favorite with holiday snackers. Decorative tins make festive containers for the colorful corn.

CANDIED CHRISTMAS POPCORN

Make two batches; tint one green and one red.

Vegetable cooking spray
16 cups popped popcorn
2 cups sugar
1/2 cup light corn syrup
2 teaspoons almond extract
1 teaspoon salt
1 teaspoon baking soda
Red and green paste food coloring

Spray inside of a 14 x 20-inch oven cooking bag with cooking spray. Place popcorn in bag. In a 2-quart microwave-safe bowl, combine sugar and corn syrup. Microwave on high power (100%) 2 minutes or until mixture boils. Stir and microwave 2 minutes longer. Stir in almond extract, salt, and baking soda; tint red or green. Pour syrup over popcorn; stir and shake until well coated. Microwave on high power 3 minutes, stirring and shaking after each minute. Spread on aluminum foil sprayed with cooking spray; cool. Store in an airtight container.
Yield: about 17 cups candied popcorn

LAYERED MEXICAN CASSEROLE

- 1 pound ground beef
- 1 jar (8 ounces) chunky salsa
- 1 package (1.5 ounces) taco seasoning
- 1 container (12 ounces) cottage cheese
- 1 package (8 ounces) shredded Cheddar cheese, divided
- 2 eggs, beaten
- 10 flour tortillas (about 7-inch diameter), divided
- 1 can (4.5 ounces) chopped green chiles, drained
- 1 can (4¼ ounces) chopped ripe olives, drained

Stirring occasionally, brown ground beef in a medium skillet over medium-high heat. Remove from heat; drain. Stir in salsa and taco seasoning.

In a medium bowl, combine cottage cheese, 1 cup Cheddar cheese, and eggs. Grease two 8-inch square baking pans. Place 4 tortillas over bottom and up sides of each pan. Spoon one-fourth of meat mixture and one-fourth of cottage cheese mixture over tortillas in each pan. Place 1 tortilla in center of each pan. Spoon remaining one-fourth of meat mixture and remaining one-fourth of cottage cheese mixture over tortilla in each pan. Sprinkle with green chiles, olives, and remaining 1 cup Cheddar cheese. Cover and store in refrigerator. Give with serving instructions.

Yield: two 8-inch casseroles, about 6 servings each

To serve: Bake covered casserole in a 350-degree oven 45 to 50 minutes or until heated through. Uncover and bake 5 minutes longer or until cheese is bubbly. Serve warm.

Surprise a busy family with a ready-made fiesta! The recipe for our spicy Layered Mexican Casserole fills two eight-inch pans.

Bursting with citrus flavor, Orange-Oatmeal Rolls begin with a hot roll mix. Our recipe makes two pans, so you can keep some for your own family, too.

ORANGE-OATMEAL ROLLS

1 package (16 ounces) hot roll mix
1 cup sweetened crunchy oat cereal
1 cup very warm orange juice (120 to 130 degrees)
2 tablespoons honey
2 tablespoons butter or margarine, melted
1 egg
1 tablespoon grated orange zest
1/2 cup coarsely ground pecans
  Vegetable cooking spray
1 cup sifted confectioners sugar
5 teaspoons orange juice

In a large bowl, combine hot roll mix and yeast from roll mix with cereal. Stir in 1 cup very warm orange juice, honey, melted butter, egg, and orange zest; stir until well blended. Stir in pecans. Turn onto a lightly floured surface and knead 3 minutes or until dough becomes smooth and elastic. Cover dough; allow to rest 10 minutes. Shape dough into eighteen 2-inch balls. Place in 2 greased 8 x 5-inch aluminum foil baking pans. Spray tops of dough with cooking spray, cover, and let rise in a warm place (80 to 85 degrees) 1 hour or until almost doubled in size.

Preheat oven to 375 degrees. Bake 15 to 20 minutes or until golden brown. Cool in pans. Combine confectioners sugar and 5 teaspoons orange juice in a small bowl; stir until smooth. Drizzle icing over rolls. Allow icing to harden. Store in an airtight container.

Yield: 2 pans rolls, 9 rolls each

Quick to prepare with fresh cranberries and frozen raspberries, tart, tangy Cranberry-Raspberry Freezer Jam makes lots of happy little gifts. Because the fruity spread keeps for up to a year in the freezer, your friends will have sweet thoughts of you long after the holidays are over.

CRANBERRY-RASPBERRY FREEZER JAM

1 cup fresh cranberries
1 package (12 ounces) frozen whole red raspberries, thawed
4 cups sugar
1 pouch (3 ounces) liquid fruit pectin
2 tablespoons freshly squeezed lemon juice

Process cranberries in a food processor until coarsely chopped. Add raspberries; process until finely chopped. Combine fruit and sugar in a large bowl. Allow fruit mixture to stand 10 minutes, stirring occasionally.

In a small bowl, combine liquid fruit pectin and lemon juice. Add pectin mixture to fruit mixture; stir constantly 3 minutes or until most of sugar dissolves. Pour into jars with lids to within 1/2 inch of tops; wipe off rims of jars. Screw on lids. Allow jam to stand at room temperature 24 hours; store in freezer. Place in refrigerator 1 hour before serving. May be refrozen. Keeps up to 3 weeks in refrigerator or up to 1 year in freezer.
Yield: about 5 cups jam

TOASTED ALMOND TOFFEE

1 cup butter
1 cup sugar
1/3 cup water
1 tablespoon light corn syrup
2 1/4 cups slivered almonds, toasted, coarsely chopped, and divided
1/2 teaspoon vanilla extract
1 cup semisweet chocolate mini chips, divided

Line 2 baking sheets with aluminum foil; grease foil. Butter sides of a very heavy large saucepan. Combine butter, sugar, water, and corn syrup in saucepan. Stirring constantly, cook over medium-low heat until sugar dissolves. Using a pastry brush dipped in hot water, wash down any sugar crystals on sides of pan. Attach a candy thermometer to pan, making sure thermometer does not touch bottom of pan. Increase heat to medium and bring to a boil. Cook, without stirring, until mixture reaches hard-crack stage (approximately 300 to 310 degrees). Test about 1/2 teaspoon mixture in ice water. Mixture will form brittle threads in ice water and will remain brittle when removed from the water. Remove from heat and stir in 1 cup almonds and vanilla. Spread mixture onto 1 prepared baking sheet. Sprinkle 1/2 cup chocolate chips over hot toffee; spread melted chocolate. Sprinkle 1/2 cup almonds over chocolate. Invert toffee onto second baking sheet. Sprinkle second side with remaining 1/2 cup chocolate chips; spread melted chocolate. Sprinkle remaining almonds over chocolate; press into chocolate. Chill 1 hour or until chocolate hardens. Break into small pieces. Store in an airtight container in a cool place.
Yield: about 1 1/2 pounds toffee

Send merry Christmas greetings with bags of Toasted Almond Toffee! The buttery chunks are coated with rich chocolate and toasted nuts.

INDEX